The Story Mandala

Finding Wholeness in a Divided World

**From Facilitators and Friends of
The Center for Renewal and Wholeness
in Higher Education**

Gathered by
Sally Z. Hare and Karen Luke Jackson
with Insights from Parker J. Palmer

Comments or questions: couragetoteach@sc.rr.com

Website:
https://www.richlandcollege.edu/cd/instruct-divisions/rlc/crwhe/
www.stilllearning.org

ISBN: 978-0-9895042-7-0

Cover photo-mandalas by Donna Bearden
(www.donnabearden.com)

Book design by Jim R. Rogers

Project created and developed by
still learning, inc.
Surfside Beach, SC

Prose Press
75 Red Maple Drive
Pawleys Island, South Carolina 29585
proseNcons@live.com

DEDICATION

To **Sue Jones** and **Ann Faulkner** and
Elaine Sullivan and **Earlene Bond**

without whom these stories would not be

and

without whom the Center for Renewal and Wholeness in
Higher Education would not be

and

with the hope that you see in these stories and
the lives of these storytellers
your legacy.

With great love and gratitude.

Before the Stories

The First Mandala: Becoming My Self

The Second Mandala: Being in Community

The Third Mandala: Wholeness as a Way of Being

After the Stories

Once Upon a Story Mandala
By Sally Z. Hare

Once upon a time.

That's the way Readers expect stories to begin. And I am a Reader. Not a writer. Not an editor. A Reader. As a Reader, I loved gathering the stories (some are poems, some are narratives, but they are ALL stories) for this book.

So that is how I will begin.

Once upon a time, the poems and essays for this book began to appear. The writers are facilitators and friends of the Center for Renewal and Wholeness in Higher Education. (You will find more about CRWHE in the last section as well as in the stories themselves.) As I read these stories, I had the sense of the writers in a circle (I even named them as a Writers Circle of Trust)—and an ever-deepening sense that these stories were creating their own intersecting circles and deserved more than an ordinary table of contents. As Karen Jackson, my co-Story Gatherer, and I looked for threads to create a structure, the image of the mandala (Sanskrit for *circle)* emerged and offered us a unique possibility for a container.

I am also a Courage and Renewal facilitator. And I have recently spent a lot of time living into the idea of thin places. Thin places, for me, are a way of naming the space where I have the best chance of nurturing the courage to seek the undivided life I want to live. In a thin place, I see my connectedness to everything around me. I see the wholeness that is my birthright gift. As I gathered these stories, I had the sense that the writers knew those kinds of thin places. There seemed to be thin places between the stories and thin places in the stories and thin places before the stories.

So we needed a design for the book that could hold all of those thin places as well as the circles that were emerging. And we needed a title. And we asked Donna Bearden, who is not only a friend of this work but also an amazing mandala artist, to help us understand how the mandala, a centuries-old image that sometimes represents the universe, might offer insight into creating a structure for our book.

Looking at Donna's images and exploring a wealth of resources, we realized that we not only had the design for our book, but also the lens we needed to see the book **and** the title. And the Story Mandala came to be.

STORIES MOVE IN CIRCLES

Now we had circles within a Circle. Advice from The Traveling Jewish Theatre in *Coming from a Great Distance* took us deeper:

> *Stories move in circles. They don't go in straight lines.*
> *So it helps if you listen in circles.*
> *There are stories inside stories and stories between stories,*
> *and finding your way through them is as easy*
> *and as hard as finding your way home.*
> *And part of the finding is the getting lost.*
> *And when you're lost, you start to look around and to listen.*

Over the years, the facilitators often complained that the work is hard to explain—and then, in the very next sentence, they would tell rich stories of how this CRWHE work or formation work or Courage work (you will also find, as you listen in circles, that it has a lot of different names!) changed their lives and the lives of their students and families and colleagues. So we invited the CRWHE facilitators and a few friends to tell their stories.

As we read and listened to the stories flowing into our mailboxes, we felt the power of the words and images to evoke our own stories – and we sensed the possibility that they would also evoke **your** stories. We remembered the wisdom of American writer and theologian, Frederick Buechner:

> *My story is important not because it is mine,*
> *but because if I tell it anything like right,*
> *the chances are you will recognize that in many ways*
> *it is also yours.*

As we discovered that mandalas are considered symbols of the connection between our inner worlds and outer reality, we found ourselves listening deeply to these stories.

And as we listened, three circles, three mandalas, emerged.

Spending time in the space inside and between and among these images immersed us in a sense of hope, of wholeness, in this world that seems so divided.

THE THREE MANDALAS

Courage Work, also called Circles of Trust, is grounded in the writing of Parker J. Palmer and his knowing that each of us has a hidden wholeness—and that the work of our lives is to make that wholeness a bit more visible, to be able to see who we really are, to find the authentic Self from which too many of us become separated in the journey of growing up. You will find Parker in many of the stories as well. And we are grateful for his gift of an essay at the beginning of each of the three mandalas.

We learned about Carl Jung's fascination with the mandala

from his writing in *Memories, Dreams, and Reflections*: "I began to understand that the goal of psychic development is the self. There is no linear evolution; there is only a circumambulation of the self." And our first section emerged, ***The First Mandala: Becoming My Self.***

Bailey Cunningham, creator of the Mandala Project, became a great resource for us through her book, *Mandala: Journey to the Center.* Cunningham wrote, "The integrated view of the world represented by the mandala, while long embraced by some Eastern religions, has now begun to emerge in Western religious and secular cultures. Awareness of the mandala may have the potential of changing how we see ourselves, our planet, and perhaps even our own life purpose." As we gathered the stories on how facilitators took their inner work into the outer world and were better able to embrace the gift of community, we could see the shape of ***The Second Mandala: Being in Community.***

A mandala represents the wholeness of the Universe, both the microcosm and the macrocosm. Jung said that a mandala symbolizes "a safe refuge of inner reconciliation and wholeness." A visual reminder of the innate order and harmony of the Universe, the mandala affirms that sense of order, harmony and wholeness that awaits us beyond our current struggles. The third circle materialized, giving us ***The Third Mandala: Wholeness as a Way of Being.***

We wanted our Story Mandala to have the same sense of hospitality and welcome that is a hallmark of our circles of trust. We wanted to invite you, our Reader, into our stories in ways that create the space for you to hear your Self. With that in mind, we have added some blank pages at the end for you to use in any way that is useful. And we have worked to keep our many years of deformation-through-academic-writing out of the way, giving credit to the teachers and poets and writers and thinkers who deepen our knowing without resorting to interruptive footnotes and bibliographies. We have also, with great intention, included the email address of each writer at the end of her essay or his poem, as an invitation to connect.

Words matter – and we encouraged our Writers to use the words that best say what they mean. If you come across a word or phrase that raises a question, we invite you into the **Words Matter** pages in the final section of our book. As you read the stories in our book, we hope you'll visit our glossary again and again; bathe in our names for things, delighting with us in knowing what we mean, and seeing the *gloss* (the root of the word glossary!) of our words, the shine, the luster.

Although the word *mandala* translates to mean "circle," a mandala has come to represent far more, to us, than a simple shape. It represents wholeness, symbolizing the organizational structure of life itself and reminding us of our connectedness to the world that extends both beyond and within our bodies and minds.

We invite you to step into The Story Mandala.

The Power of Story: The Truth of Our Lives
By Elaine Sullivan

*If you could imagine the most incredible story ever,
it would be less incredible than the story of our being
here alive on this earth. Ironically, it is not "just" a
story: it's the truth of our lives. Yet it takes us so long
to see where we are along the path of our soul's story.
And it takes us even longer to see who we are. The
single most important gift you can give yourself is the
invitation to awaken to who you are and where you
have landed.*

John O'Donohue, *The Question Holds the Lantern*

In the late 60's, I was working at the University of Stevens
Point, Wisconsin. I had just left religious life where I had been
for over 17 years. That transition was a challenging experience:
fear, hope, excitement. I was beginning my own single life as
a counselor at the university where I was also director of a
women's residence hall.

Early in my work I became aware of how many of our students
gathered at bars to make their social connections. I was appalled
at the practice of using alcohol to seek connections and asked
myself what I could do to help students connect. I started a
process in my hall where 30 students, male and female, were
invited to my living room to spend three hours sharing stories.

The students never wanted to go home after spending an
evening with their stories. Word spread like wildfire on the
campus; soon I was offering this experience three evenings

each week. It was with these young people that I began to understand the power of story: through stories we recognize, in a deep and profound way, that we are all connected.

A few years later, I married Joseph Sullivan, a former priest, and we moved to Chicago where I took a counseling position at Oakton Community College. The vice president asked me to do something to support and encourage women who were returning to college as young and middle-aged adults, saying, "I have no money for this."

I jokingly responded: "I used to walk on water, but I don't any more. I will see what I can do."

I re-designed a psychology course for women returning to school based on what I had learned from writing my own autobiography for my graduate work. The experience of writing my story was extremely powerful for me. I began to see many patterns in my life that I had been unaware of: some positive, some negative. At that time in the early 70's, there was very little written on the power of story, particularly on autobiographical writing.

I intuitively knew this work would attract women. I planned the course so that in 16 weeks the students would write their autobiographies and share their stories. Word spread very quickly about this course, and soon I was offering four to 12 sections each semester. As this class grew in popularity, I began to train other teachers to hold a space for this kind of work.

Little did I realize what incredible territory I was entering. The stories of these women opened my eyes like no previous experience.

Now, 50 years later, having listened to hundreds of stories

(actually I have read and worked with over 2500 students in this process), I have come to understand the power of owning our story and not letting it own us.

THE POWER OF STORY MEETS THE POWER OF PARKER PALMER

In 1980 I moved with my husband and two sons to Dallas, Texas, where I worked on the faculty at Richland College. Under the outstanding leadership of its president, Stephen Mittelstet, I was invited to continue my work with story while I directed the Adult Resource Center. During that time we had an "Uncommittee" which met monthly across all disciplines to read and discuss books. When we read Parker Palmer's book, *To Know as We Are Known,* I was thrilled to find someone whose writing supported my story work. Finally I had found someone in higher education who recognized the value of subjective as well as objective learning.

I had been criticized frequently for offering a fluff course with no substance. That criticism never deterred me because I saw what my course evoked in the student, affirming my deep knowing of the importance of story work in human development. At this same time I was working on the Board of Directors for the National Wellness Institute (NWI) where I used the sharing of personal stories to encourage leaders in the Wellness Movement to understand the depth of the mind, body, spirit connection. Research strongly pointed to the possibility that isolation and illness negatively affect our health, while connection, intimacy and community positively affect our health.

Wellness at that time was focused primarily on physical fitness, so I offered workshops on story at the annual conferences to broaden that understanding. My sessions were always filled, and the feedback from participants amazed me. I was honored, years later, to receive the Halbert Dunn Award for my contributions to the Wellness Movement, primarily that of owning the power in your own story.

At one of my NWI keynote addresses I spoke about Parker's work, and an audience member from the Fetzer Institute told me that Parker was developing a program to prepare facilitators to offer his work; she suggested I contact him. I already felt deeply committed to learn more from him and wanted to study with him if I ever had the opportunity. The Dallas District, where I was working, brought Parker in as a consultant, and as it turned out, a group of us were invited to the Fetzer Institute for a retreat with him!

Out of that experience, I joined a group of faculty in writing *To Teach With Soft Eyes*, a series of essays on how we used Parker's work in our classrooms. I was thrilled with what was happening on our campus. Soon after that, in 1998, I was invited, as part of a national group of educators, to a weekend retreat at Fetzer under Parker's leadership. Ten of us were selected to continue our work with Parker to be prepared to facilitate this new work he was calling *teacher formation*. As part of that, I participated in a Clearness Committee as a focus person to deepen my discernment about my work with story. Sally Z. Hare was the clerk in that committee that began my journey in this work. Her support was a breath of fresh air as I realized that all my years of work with story had prepared me for this deepening experience.

I relished every opportunity to learn with this group as we worked with Parker. The heart of this formation work, just as the work I had created for returning women, was about the Self: Who am I? I learned much more about creating safe space for the soul to show up; about holding the space to embrace the paradoxes of wounds and gifts, shadow and light, weakness and strength, limitations and possibilities. I learned that reflecting on our personal stories and the stories of others opens the heart to discover the uniqueness and beauty hidden in the caverns of our souls. Listening deeply to ourselves and to others, we become more open to who we really are, to our True Self.

THE ADDED GIFT OF MEMORY

Memory reclaimed in storytelling is one of the beautiful aspects of the deep limitless space within us all. As we age we have the opportunity to gift ourselves through harvesting and integrating those memories. **Your** memory will often unlock a memory in **me**—a moment of deep connection. Harvesting memories has always been a critical process in my autobiographical work: participants would come alive as they shared memories and sometimes metaphors. I remember one of my students at the end of class asking for metaphors of the body to describe her and receiving beautiful ones. Then she went home to her four children and asked them what metaphor of the body they would give her. Without missing a beat, her 11-year-old daughter said, "Mother, you are an ovary!"

"What do you mean?" she asked her daughter.

"Well, Mom, you only let your kid out about once a month." That single Mom shared with us that she was radically changed after that: she realized that she was oblivious to the fact that she played with her kids only one weekend each month; the rest of the time she worked.

Working with the imagination through metaphor and imagery has always been a delight. O'Donohue has written, *"When you begin to sense that your imagination is the place where you are most divine, you feel called to clean out of your mind all the worn and shabby furniture of thought. You wish to refurbish yourself with the living imagination so that you can begin to see, so that your thoughts can become what Meister Eckhart calls 'inner senses.'"* Parker's work has opened me to new ways to use the imagination through story, images, metaphors. Poetry opens our hearts and souls to see with new eyes and hear with new ears. Metaphors, such as the metaphors of the seasons, invite us to see more clearly the process of growth and transformation in our lives. In many stories I have witnessed the cocoon-to-butterfly process, especially in times of transition, in times of loss, in times of grief, in times of letting go, in times of change, in times of pain.

THE INTERSECTION OF FACILITATOR PREPARATION AND THE POWER OF STORY

I have worked with the Center for Renewal and Wholeness in Higher Education (CRWHE) for many years, preparing facilitators for this work. I have also had the rich opportunity to mentor many facilitators and attend their first retreats. I consider this to be one of the greatest gifts of my life as, over and over, I have seen the power of storytelling, the opening of the imagination through poetry, art, story, film, music and nature. In this deepening work our stories hold the possibility of insights that invite transformation in ourselves and others.

When we began the work, we started as the Center for Formation in the Community College. Community college work is done **in** community **for** the community. Now that we have expanded the Center to include others, CRWHE facilitators not only work in community colleges and other institutions of higher education, but also in other areas such as corporate America, hospice care and churches. I believe that writing and reading the stories of others will inspire us to continue building on the work that has been done.

Parker writes that "at every stage of a movement there is both the power to help change happen and encouragement for disheartened souls. Wherever we are on this journey, a step taken to renew our spirits may turn out to be a step towards wholeness and integrity and a step to strengthen our community."

I believe writing and sharing our stories is one of those steps.

In the opening pages of this book, Sally (yes, the same Sally who clerked on that long-ago Clearness Committee) lifted up the words of Frederick Buechner to remind us that our stories are not important because they are ours, but because our stories are also **your** stories.

As you enter The Story Mandala, I share John O'Donohue's wise words:

*it is not **just** a story: it's **the truth of our lives**.*

The Touchstones

Of the Center for Renewal and Wholeness in
Higher Education

As you enter the Story Mandala, you will find many of the
writers mention The Touchstones. These guidelines are
used in Courage and Renewal settings, in circles of trust,
even in meetings and workshops, to mark the boundaries
for safe space. Prepared by formation facilitators with
considerable help from the writings of Judy Brown, Parker
Palmer and the Dialogue Group, The Touchstones offer
you a portal into The Story Mandala.

Be 100% present, extending and presuming welcome.
Set aside the usual distractions of things undone from
yesterday, things to do tomorrow. Bring all of yourself
to the work. We all learn most effectively in spaces that
welcome us. Welcome others to this place and this work,
and presume that you are welcomed as well.

Listen deeply. Listen intently to what is said; listen to
the feelings beneath the words. As Quaker writer Douglas
Steere puts it, "Holy listening—to 'listen' another's soul
into life, into a condition of disclosure and discovery may
be almost the greatest service that any human being ever
performs for another." Listen to yourself as well as to
others. Strive to achieve a balance between listening and
reflecting, speaking and acting.

It is never "share or die." You will be invited to share in pairs, small groups, and in the large group. The invitation is exactly that. *You* will determine the extent to which you want to participate in our discussions and activities.

No fixing. Each of us is here to discover our own truths, to listen to our own inner teacher, to take our own inner journey. We are *not* here to set someone else straight, or to help right another's wrong, to "fix" what we perceive as broken in another member of the group.

Suspend judgment. Set aside your judgments. By creating a space between judgments and reactions, we can listen to the other, and to ourselves, more fully.

Identify assumptions. Our assumptions are usually invisible to us, yet they undergird our worldview. By identifying our assumptions, we can then set them aside and open our viewpoints to greater possibilities.

Speak your truth. You are invited to say what is in your heart, trusting that your voice will be heard and your contribution respected. Your truth may be different from, even the opposite of, what another person in the circle has said. Yet speaking your truth is simply that: it is not debating with, or correcting, or interpreting what another has said. *Own* your truth by remembering to speak only for yourself. Using the first person "I" rather than "you" or "everyone" clearly communicates the personal nature of your expression.

Respect silence. Silence is a rare gift in our busy world. After someone has spoken, take time to reflect without immediately filling the space with words. This applies to the speaker as well: be comfortable leaving your words to

THE STORY MANDALA

resound in the silence, without refining or elaborating on what you have just said. This process allows others time to fully listen before reflecting on their own reactions.

Maintain confidentiality. Create a safe space by respecting the confidential nature and content of discussions held in the formation circle. Allow what is said in the circle to remain there.

When things get difficult, turn to wonder. If you find yourself disagreeing with another, becoming judgmental, or shutting down in defense, try turning to wonder: "I wonder what brought her to this place?" "I wonder what my reaction teaches me?" "I wonder what he's feeling right now?"

Practice slowing down. As Thomas Merton and others have cautioned, the pace of modern life can cause violent damage to the soul. By intentionally practicing slowing down, we strengthen our ability to extend non-violence to others—and to ourselves.

The First Mandala

Becoming My Self

Finding True Self:
Choosing to Live Undivided
By Parker J. Palmer

"There is in all things ... a hidden wholeness."

Thomas Merton, the Trappist monk and mystic who wrote these words, was speaking of the human world as well as the world of nature. But in our everyday lives, Merton's words can sound like wishful thinking. Afraid that our inner light will be extinguished, or our inner darkness exposed, we hide our true identities and become separated from our own souls. We end up leading divided lives, far removed from our birthright wholeness.

The divided life comes in many and varied forms. To cite just a few examples, it is the life we lead when:

- We refuse to invest ourselves in our work, diminishing its quality and distancing ourselves from those it is meant to serve

- We make our living at jobs that violate our basic values, even when survival does not absolutely demand it

- We remain in settings or relationships that steadily kill off our spirit

- We harbor secrets to achieve personal gain at the expense of other people

- We hide our beliefs from those who disagree with us to avoid conflict, challenge, and change

- We conceal our true identities for fear of being criticized, shunned, or attacked

My knowledge of the divided life comes first from personal experience. A "still, small voice" speaks the truth about me, my work, or the world. I hear it and yet act as if I did not. I withhold a personal gift that might serve a good end or commit myself to a project that I do not really believe in. I keep silent on an issue I should address or actively break faith with one of my own convictions. I deny my inner darkness, giving it more power over me, or I project it onto other people, creating "enemies" where none exist.

I pay a steep price when I live a divided life, feeling fraudulent, anxious about being found out, and depressed by the fact that I am denying my own selfhood. The people around me pay a price as well, for now they walk on ground made unstable by my dividedness. How can I affirm another's integrity when I deny my own? A fault line runs down the middle of my life, and whenever it cracks open—divorcing my words and actions from the truth I hold within—hings around me get shaky and start to fall apart.

The more dividedness we perceive in each other, the less safe and sane we feel. Every day as we interact with family, friends, acquaintances, and strangers, we ask ourselves, "Is this person the same on the inside as he or she seems to be on the outside?"

Children ask this about their parents, students about their teachers, employees about their supervisors, patients about their physicians, and citizens about their political leaders. When the answer is yes, we relax, believing that we are in the presence of integrity and feeling secure enough to invest ourselves in the relationship and all that surrounds it.

But when the answer is no, we go on high alert. If our roles were more deeply informed by the truth that is in our souls, the general level of sanity and safety would rise dramatically.

A teacher who shares his or her identity with students is more effective than one who lobs factoids at them from behind a wall. A supervisor who leads from personal authenticity gets better work out of people than one who leads from a script. A doctor who invests selfhood in his or her practice is a better healer than one who treats patients at arm's length. A politician who brings personal integrity into leadership helps us reclaim the popular trust that distinguishes true democracy from its cheap imitations.

THE PATHOLOGY OF THE DIVIDED LIFE

How shall we understand the pathology of the divided life? If we approach it as a problem to be solved by "raising the ethical bar"—exhorting each other to jump higher and meting out tougher penalties to those who fall short—we may feel more virtuous for a while, but we will not address the problem at its source.

The divided life, at bottom, is not a failure of ethics; it is a failure of human wholeness. Doctors who are dismissive of patients, politicians who lie to voters, executives who cheat retirees out of their savings, clerics who rob children of their well-being—these people, for the most part, do not lack ethical knowledge or convictions. But they have a well-rehearsed habit of holding their own knowledge and beliefs at great remove from the living of their lives.

The divided life may be endemic, but wholeness is always a choice. "Being whole" is a self-evident good, and yet time after time we choose against wholeness by slipping into a familiar pattern of evasion:

- First comes denial: surely what I have seen about myself cannot be true!

- Next comes equivocation: the inner voice speaks softly, and truth is a subtle, slippery thing, so how can I be sure of what my soul is saying?

- Then fear: if I let that inner voice dictate the shape of my life, what price might I have to pay in a world that sometimes punishes authenticity?

- Next comes cowardice: the divided life may be destructive, but at least I know the territory, while what lies beyond it is terra incognita.

- Then comes avarice: in some situations, I am rewarded for being willing to stifle my soul.

The divided life is a wounded life, and the soul keeps calling us to heal the wound. Ignore that call, and we find ourselves trying to numb our pain with an anesthetic of choice, be it substance abuse, overwork, consumerism, or mindless media noise. Such anesthetics are easy to come by in a society that wants to keep us divided and unaware of our pain—for the divided life that is pathological for individuals can serve social systems well, especially when it comes to those functions that are morally dubious.

CHOOSING TO LIVE DIVIDED NO MORE

No one wants to suffer the penalties that come from choosing to live divided no more. But there can be no greater suffering than living a lifelong lie. As we move closer to the truth that lives within us—aware that in the end what will matter most is knowing that we stayed true to ourselves—institutions start losing their sway over our lives.

This does not mean we must abandon institutions. In fact, when we live by the soul's imperatives, we gain the courage to serve institutions more faithfully, to help them resist their tendency to default on their own missions. It is not easy work, rejoining soul and role. The poet Rilke—who wrote about childhood's "wingèd energy of delight"—writes about the demands of adulthood in the final stanza of the same poem:

Take your practiced powers and stretch them out
until they span the chasm between two contradictions. . .
For the god wants to know himself in you.

Living integral lives is daunting. We must achieve a complex integration that spans the contradictions between inner and outer reality, that supports both personal integrity and the common good. No, it is not easy work. But as Rilke suggests, by doing it, we offer what is sacred within us to the life of the world.

Parker J. Palmer is a writer, teacher and activist who works independently on issues in education, community, leadership, spirituality, and social change. Founder and Senior Partner of the Center for Courage & Renewal, he has authored 11 books, including **The Courage to Teach, Let Your Life Speak, A Hidden Wholeness, Healing the Heart of Democracy,** and most recently, **On the Brink of Everything: Grace, Gravity & Getting Old.** He holds a Ph.D. in sociology from the University of California at Berkeley, and his work has been recognized with 13 honorary doctorates and the William Rainey Harper Award, whose previous recipients include Margaret Mead, Elie Wiesel, Paolo Freire.

The Sacred Work of Death Doula and Teacher: Learning to Stand in the Tragic Gap

By Jude Higgins

"The only way out is through; the only way through is in."

That quote by Robert Frost (and some say inspired by Macbeth), with an additional tag line from shamanic traditions, is now forever embedded in my body. For me, this has become my mantra for living an undivided, authentic life.

My work as a CRWHE facilitator has directly informed my journey; however, my journey began long before I became a facilitator, with my very first renewal and wholeness retreat. The Faculty Development Staff at my college encouraged me to attend that retreat, and I went without ever realizing that I truly **was** seeking renewal and wholeness.

Faculty in colleges and universities are never taught how to teach. We become "experts" in our field and are then sent out to transfer that information to students—such a shame, because most of us have no idea how to make that happen.

With regard to taking on a classroom full of students, I recall feeling more prepared than most because my first career was in dance, and although I danced professionally, I also taught on the side. However, a room full of artists is a very different beast. In the artistic space, there is an immediate command of respect the moment a student walks through the door. Students in an artistic space enter with a sense of admiration—they come to study with a particular artist because of the reputation that precedes them.

Although there is the rare exception, this is typically not the case in colleges or universities. Usually, faculty classes fill because they are seen as easy or they fit the student's schedule. Needless to say, mine were no different; in my first few years of teaching student relations were problematic at best. The most common comment in my student evaluations was that I was *unapproachable*. I would read the same word over and over and brush it off. I would justify my behavior by thinking that students were afraid of someone in a position of authority (which they are, but I failed to realize that it was my job to assuage that fear), or I assumed they were making an excuse not to come during my office hours for help; after all, I knew that I genuinely cared and was really nice—almost a pushover… Obviously, they had no idea what they were talking about. Or did they?

My journey in renewal and wholeness gave me the tools I needed to transform my teaching, heal my childhood and familial wounds, journey through a difficult and painful divorce, and find my passion and current calling in the service work (as a death doula), which is the focus of this article. As I said, this work has given me many tools, but I will discuss the one that has been the most significant for me in all areas of my life—learning to embrace my uncomfortable feelings when I stand in the tragic gap.

STANDING IN THE TRAGIC GAP

The biggest transformative experience I had through my work with renewal and wholeness (and I would venture to say my most important tool to date) is the ability to exist in the tragic gap—that uncomfortable place of in-between. I've learned ways to think about holding the tension between what is—the difficulty, the darkness, the hardness, and the shadow of it all, and what I know to be possible—what could and should be (in a realistic sense, not in an idealistic one). I continue the practice of standing in this space without moving to one side or the other.

As Parker Palmer writes in *A Hidden Wholeness*, standing in the gap is the ability to be in this space without being drawn into the side of "corrosive cynicism" or falling into "irrelevant idealism" (as Palmer says, "too much possibility causes us to fly above the battle"). Either binary end of the spectrum takes us to the same place of immobility, and as a result, we disengage; we are rendered unable to move.

The question is, how do we learn to stand there?

And the answer is through this sacred work of renewal and wholeness.

Through this work, we learn to reach deep inside ourselves and develop practices that open our hearts, minds, and invite our gentle, quiet souls into active being. We slowly begin to hear our souls with more clarity, eventually even engaging in soulful conversation.

It has taken a long time for me to be able to listen to my soul. My soul whispers, and so often, I'd talk over it, or brush aside any advice it gave me. Learning to truly hear the whisper of my soul has been an invaluable achievement, and I credit this work.

Experiencing the paradox of doing inner work (the examined life) in community is one way the tragic gap is modeled. Inner work is how we face ourselves but doing it in community is important because we are so clever and able when it comes to self-delusion. Turns out that it is really difficult to determine when we are operating from shadow (acting and responding because we are filled with resentment, anger, jealousy). But in the gentle, safe, space of community, we can check and ultimately correct our own self-perceptions. One beautiful aspect of community is that we all come from different perspectives, humanistic, spiritual, etc., and when we hear numerous voices in a circle of trust, each has the ability to touch our soul and generate growth in a unique way.

This work teaches us practices that help open our hearts so we can stand in the tragic gap—standing and holding what appear to be radical opposites. This is an important quality for any person who wants to create positive change in our world. And this is what led me to my service work as a death doula.

End-of-life doulas help individuals and families as they move through the process of dying, and every aspect of working and helping individuals and families with an end-of-life transition comes down to the ability to stand in the tragic gap, to hold space. Many times, individuals want to hold loved ones here, or at the other extreme, push them toward the light because the process of death is uncomfortable, and it is difficult to be in that space for any length of time.

THE ALIGNMENT OF THE WORK

The end-of-life doula helps everyone stand in the tragic gap that exists between life and death; the doula is trained to hold space and help people stand there, and the renewal and wholeness work has been a critical piece in my training. In fact, I have been amazed at how closely aligned the sacred work of a death doula is to those who facilitate renewal and wholeness circles.

Another example is the way in which the death doula is trained in creating a space for quiet souls to emerge. End-of-life doulas are trained to be comfortable with silence, to listen, to ask open-ended questions, and to explore issues that come up when people know they are facing the end of life (guilt, shame, regrets, unfinished business). Much of this work is similar to the work I have done when facilitating renewal and wholeness circles. The renewal and wholeness work is the basis and actually informs the sacred work of a death doula. This work has been instrumental for me in terms of living an undivided life.

I have found my calling for the service work I do, and I am now training others to become end-of-life doulas. This work has been instrumental in that, and I think it has the profound ability to change the world in which we live for the better.

Oh, and in case you are wondering, my student evaluations no longer include the word *unapproachable*. I continuously receive letters of praise and thanks from my students, and I recently won the Teaching Excellence Award at my college.

I am forever growing and learning, continuing to live into the meaning of "the only way out is through; the only way through is in." I credit this work for helping me to make these significant steps toward learning to stand in the tragic gap in order to live an undivided life.

Jude Higgins is an Associate Professor of Anthropology at Salt Lake Community College, and a Ph.D. Candidate in Educational Leadership & Policy at the University of Utah. She is also an End of Life Doula and trains others in this work for the company HELD: help from an end of life doula. She lives in Salt Lake City, Utah and can be contacted through mydeathdoula.com

Dear Mr. Hamrin

By Donna Bearden

Do you remember that day I came into your office? I was 16. It was the second week of school. I had just been released from the hospital with severe stomach pains. I needed to lighten my schedule. Concerned, you commented on the schedule, made the changes, asked about my many extra-curricular activities, and then you asked a question I have never forgotten. You looked me square in the eye and said, *"What are you trying to prove?"*

I didn't have the words to tell you that things were not so good at home. I thought my home was normal. Doesn't every kid until they get out in the world and can compare? I just knew it was someplace I didn't like to be. I took the hardest courses because that's what was expected. I used activities to stay away as much as possible.

I couldn't explain all that to you. I didn't figure it out until decades later.

School was my refuge. Busyness was my drug of choice. Intellectualism was my family's theme and I could never measure up. I just wasn't. Intellectual, I mean. We don't need to rehash the details. It's your question I want to get back to. I finally have an answer. Do you still want to know?

I went to college. Got married. Had a career. Had children. But I was an addict, don't you see? An addict to busyness. It was what I did to keep myself from falling down a deep, dark well. I kept trying to become that intellectual I "had potential" to be. Worked hard. Very hard. Life was serious. So many problems. I read. I researched. I knew how to solve problems. Just give me one and I'll tell you how.

You were my math teacher a few years before you were my high school counselor. You knew I could solve problems. You knew I had potential.

What a loaded word that is. *Potential.* An underhanded compliment. It always means you're not quite there. I always had a lot of *potential.*

I'm going to skip forward a few decades. The details aren't so important, and I want to answer your question before you lose interest. I did a lot of stuff. Accomplished a lot. Advanced in my career. Got a couple of advanced degrees. But that *potential* thing was always out of reach. I knew that if I just tried hard enough, read enough, studied enough, I would put it altogether.

The problem was I didn't exactly know what "it" was. There was no joy in Mudville. Something was missing. I knew that by the deep, dark well that was always waiting for me if I slowed down. I did what I knew to do: work hard. Stay busy. Be serious. Solve problems.

In trying to fix everything (my family, my field of work, anyone who presented me with a problem), I also tried to fix myself. Read every self-help book I could get my hands on. Got trained in efficiency and time management. I'm telling you, I was relentless in my search to be the perfect…. The perfect what? I don't know. I just know I was trying awfully hard.

One day I picked up a book like nothing else I had ever read. All those books that told me how to get my life together, how to manage time, how to mold and shape children, how to get employees to do what you needed them to do—this was a book that challenged everything I had learned. Well, not quite everything. That is an exaggeration and I'm trying to be as truthful as possible.

This author told me I didn't have to fix people. I didn't have to advise. I didn't have to set anyone straight. And, in fact, when I did so, I was short-circuiting that person's learning. I was discounting that person. He was capable. She was capable. It was not my job to save the world or anyone in it. WHAT??

Mr. Hamrin, have you ever had an *Aha!* moment? You know, one of those times when something clicks in place and you know beyond a shadow of a doubt that you have witnessed a truth. That's what happened for me that day. This huge, heavy weight had been lifted from my shoulders. HUGE. HEAVY. I had carried it around for 40 years. That's how hard I tried, Mr. Hamrin. To prove to you, to my parents, to my bosses and employees, to my neighbors, to anyone I met that I was capable of living up to my *potential*.

I read those words in *A Hidden Wholeness*. I saw the endnote about further training. I booked a flight and was at Bainbridge Island the next month for my first Courage retreat. I was HUNGRY, don't you see?

But I'm only beginning to tell you about transformation. That was the wake-up call. Someone was knocking on my cocoon and saying, "All-y, all-y out's in free." For you see, I lived inside the safety of my cocoon, spun from my own beliefs and assumptions of the world and who I was supposed to be in that world. Beliefs and assumptions I had absorbed from the big people who had had so much power over me and who knew about potential and all that.

That first weekend retreat left me in tears. No, don't get me wrong, Mr. Hamrin. They weren't sad or angry tears. They were tears from deep down. Maybe all-the-way-to-my-toes tears.

These people were not trying to fix me, mold me, shape me, teach me, praise me, control me, be amazed at my potential, or anything else that even hinted at my needing to perform. They simply wanted to see me. The real me. The me behind the masks and costumes and pretenses. It was a deepening of the feeling I got from reading the book. Someone sees me. *Someone. Sees. Me.*

Synchronistically, I learned about all the opportunities for further involvement right in my own backyard. So much transformational work going on in the Dallas-Fort Worth metroplex. I signed up for another weekend retreat. And a year-long seasonal retreat. And and and. Even now the tears come to my eyes as I tell you about it. Do you understand what it's like to live behind masks, to take the busyness drug to keep from falling down the well? And after putting so much time and effort and determination into head pursuits (intellectualism), to hear the small, quiet voice deep inside asking, "What about me? Did you forget me? Can I please come out and play?"

Even my head was lopsided. Serious. Analytical. All what they call left-brain thinking. Here's an irony for you: *I collected books on creativity*. I studied it like a researcher. But I wouldn't let myself play because, well, it seemed too much like playing.

There is a happy ending to this story. I promise. Maybe it's time to cut to the chase. I think you've got enough of the idea of where I came from. And the importance of finding a community experience where I felt seen and heard not for the masks I wore or the roles I played, but for the ME deep inside.

Mr. Hamrin, if you could have been a fly on the wall, you could have watched the transformation. Little by little, my little girl, my little self who was really my Big Self, shyly came out.

What do you want to do, Little Girl?

I want to dance.
I want to paint.
I want to play outdoors.
I want to be creative.
I want to write heart-felt things,
not research papers,
footnotes,
bibliographies.

Let the Little Girl dance.

Slowly she stepped forward. *I* stepped forward. I can claim her now. I DO claim her now. I have always been a photographer. That has been a passion among all the serious stuff. There were times the camera had to go up on a shelf, but I always came back to it. It was a faithful and patient friend, and like a long-time friend, we could pick up where we left off.

My camera came out bigger and bolder.

I need to stop here for a moment to tell you I could not have done any of this on my own. That's an important point in this story. When I was a kid, around four years old, we were about to cross a street. My mother said something about holding hands. I declared I would hold my own hand, and I did. My mother repeated that story occasionally about her daughter who was so determined to do everything on her own. She was proud of it and never saw the pain beneath it. I learned early that I was on my own. So, what I'm trying to tell you, Mr. Hamrin, is that letting other people in was not easy for me. Getting to the point of **knowing** and then **acknowledging** that I couldn't have done any of this on my own was a huge step. Gigantic.

Yes, my camera came out bigger and bolder this time. Then there was that "accidental" stumbling onto a website about photo-mandalas. Mandalas had intrigued me because of Carl Jung's use of drawing mandalas to go deeper into the subconscious. I tried drawing a few, and then stumbled onto this photo-mandala website. Oh my gosh did I have fun! I started creating photo-mandalas left and right.

About that time, I was working with a very wise woman, a Courage facilitator, who was helping me delve deeper into all that muck and mud and grimy stuff that was keeping me, the real me, from breaking free of that protective cocoon. The cocoon inside the guarded castle behind the moat filled with alligators. Yes, maybe I exaggerate. But no, maybe I don't. Elaine Sullivan is one of the wisest people I have ever met. *Wise*. Look it up sometime. It has nothing to do with intellectualism. It has more to do with thinking through your heart.

Elaine had me do a lot of writing. (I'm tempted to put a footnote here, a reference, but I'm done with that research mode. I'll just say if you want to know more about writing to get at deep emotions, look up James W. Pennebaker. He's done a lot of good work in that area.)

Every day I wrote, and then I went to my computer and selected a photograph to create a photo-mandala. I have thousands of images. (That is not an exaggeration.) I would flip through them and select one without thinking. Just something that caught my eye. I would create a mandala and somehow that mandala would echo what I had written. I can't explain it. I only know that things became clearer. Something popped out or quietly tapped me on the shoulder, and I knew through my eyes, my heart, my art what I hadn't understood through my logic.

Mr. Hamrin, that's how the Mandala Messages got started. I would pair a mandala with a quote. Sometimes I'd use someone else's writing, but I finally got to the point where I trusted my own voice more, and I wanted to put my own words out there. Thanks to Cindy Johnson, another sensitive and skilled facilitator, the Courage network began sending these messages out twice a month as a regular mailing. It has grown from there. Now I send them out every week to a regular email list.

But that's not all. That was a beginning. One among many.

Someone else saw the mandalas and said they would be pretty on silk scarves. Wow! That's an idea! Research skills do come in handy. Yes, there was a company. Yes, I could do it. Yes, I did it. Yes, I can even say they were beautiful!

We moved to Colorado where people are more casual and there wasn't much market for silk scarves. Hmmm. How about tiles, trivets, Christmas ornaments? The cottage industry grew and grew. Greeting cards, a book, prints, a couple galleries. And now a blog.

I believe there is an artist in each one of us just waiting to come out. Not necessarily a capital-A artist, but an artist all the same. We are each creative in our own unique ways. I was hungry for my artist to come out. I had kept mine at bay for so long, thinking I had to be smart, accomplished in "serious" stuff, admired for my problem-solving abilities and my multi-tasking. But, Mr. Hamrin, all I had to do was slow down to feel the emptiness, the loneliness, the aching inside. If anyone was a poster child for living divided, I think I was in the running.

Was. Past tense.

This year I was asked to do a one-person show of my mandala art. The pieces are big, some as big as four feet tall! Printed on metal and canvas and wood. There will be more than two dozen of them, and the exhibit will be up for three months starting in October. Can you believe that?! I couldn't. But it's happening! I'd love for you to come see it, Mr. Hamrin. I'd love to sit down with you and tell you I can finally answer the question you asked so long ago.

What are you trying to prove? You asked.

In a nutshell I was trying to prove I was something I wasn't. And that, even under the best of circumstances, is an impossible equation to prove. Either I'm extremely persistent or a very slow learner. It took me a long, long time, but at last, with the help of a supportive community, I broke through the cocoon. What I needed more than anything else was unconditional acceptance so I would feel safe enough to be who I was deep inside. That is what a circle of trust and all the members and teachers and facilitators of circles offered me, and what I slowly and cautiously grew to trust.

It's still a little hard for me to claim, Mr. Hamrin, so I'm going to say it quietly. I'll whisper it in your ear. *I am a creative artist.*

But wait! Hold the phone! The transition was bigger than that.

I AM A CREATIVE ARTIST!

There!

With love,
Donna

P.S. You'll be happy to know that the well is gone. I won't tell you that everything's hunky-dory every single day. I have set-backs. Addictions are like that. It's a steep learning curve requiring lots of practice to change life-long habits. But I have support. Tons of it. When I finally let go of my own hand, I could hardly believe how many offered to hold it. I just had to ask.

Donna Bearden, life-long learner, lives in Loveland, Colorado, with an incredibly supportive husband. She is following her bliss: hiking, photographing, riding her bike, writing, and creating mandala art. Visit her website at www.donnabearden.com (you will find a bit more information on that in the final section of this book), or contact her at donna.bearden14@gmail.com

Being Who I am Supposed To Be

By Earlene Bond

"We are born perfectly who we are supposed to be."

I first heard Parker Palmer say these words while I was working in the Staff Development Office of Richland College in Dallas, Texas. I didn't realize then that those words would become the map for my journey.

That journey began in 1998 when I was asked to provide "behind-the-scene support" for Sue Jones who was facilitating programs on campus grounded in Palmer's writing. An extra perk: I could attend retreats such as *The Courage to Teach* and *Let Your Life Speak* as a participant. There I became fascinated with what I saw happening in the lives of faculty and staff and knew I wanted to be a part of this work.

When I heard that a soon-to-be Center for Formation in Community Colleges would be advertising for support staff, I had conflicting emotions. The new position was calling my name, but I'd been at Richland as a student and employee for fifteen years. People at the college were family. I'd found a comfortable place to learn, work, and help create a greater sense of community. Leaving my current job, where I'd been the "start-up" employee, would be like leaving my baby. However, I was fascinated with the idea of reaching other community colleges with Palmer's work. What to do?

At one of our campus retreats, I asked to be a focus person so I could explore that question in a clearness committee setting. The committee members asked good open and honest questions, and I came away knowing it was time to leave my comfort zone. In 2001, when the newly created Center (now the Center for Renewal and Wholeness in Higher Education) advertised for a Senior Executive Assistant, I applied. The day I was offered the position, a new leg of my journey began.

I moved from the Richland campus to the Center's home in downtown Dallas. The city was building DART, its new Dallas Area Rapid Transit system, but it wasn't complete to my neighborhood. Each day I drove to Richland, parked my car and boarded a bus to the DART station, then climbed upon a railway which transported me to the city's urban center. From there it was a short walk to the Dallas Community College District office where much of our grant writing, program planning, and recruiting took place.

MY THREE TEACHERS

Now, almost 20 years later, I realize that supporting Sue Jones and Ann Faulkner and Elaine Sullivan as they led retreats and trained facilitators, expanded my horizons; each one became a teacher for me on my journey to "being who I was supposed to be." These three women, who led the Center's work, have had an impact on my life that's hard to describe. They've taught me by their examples of integrity, responsibility, and authenticity. They not only "talk the talk;" they truly "walk the walk."

Elaine's gift of storytelling with wit and humor often reminded me to "take myself lightly." Active and lively, even now in her eighties, she became a role model for many of us who sat in her circles. Sue's careful planning, what we call "the work before the work," and her ability to make people feel welcome inspired our entire team as we began to introduce formation work to faculty, staff, and administrators from community colleges across the nation. Ann's artistic talents and attention to detail greatly enhanced workshops and retreat designs. Being housed in the same office, I found myself surrounded by positive energy and engaged in meaningful work.

Looking back at my journey, I understand that we choose to react to what happens in our lives, "the good, the bad, and the ugly," and that response is an important part of what makes us who we are today. My choices about how to react changed greatly as I engaged in the new work. Fundamental were the Touchstones, guidelines used in our circles to create safe space. They helped me learn in all aspects of my life how to live and interact with others with respect and dignity, especially those with whom I disagreed. For example, as a mother of three grown daughters, I spent a lot of years trying to "fix" them, or so I thought. After learning about the Touchstones, I became aware of how little I paid attention to what they were saying and how judgmental I could become at times. As I listened more and tried to fix them less, these young women grew up to be fantastic adults.

Another skill I picked up was the art of asking open, honest questions, which Parker modeled on many occasions. I've found this practice useful in dealing with family, friends, and co-workers. I also value silence now when before it felt strange. And there are days that I have to remember to suspend judgment, and when things get difficult, turn to wonder.

Listening deeply in and out of retreat circles became a gift I could offer others. In turn, when someone deeply listens to me, I feel extremely blessed. Finally, drawing on Elaine's teachings, I've turned to humor to help me cope with challenges along the way.

Never have I needed humor more than six years ago when I started having health problems. First, I lost my sense of smell and didn't realize it until my daughter asked me to check her son's diaper. I bent down to sniff and couldn't detect anything. When she came over, before she even looked, she gagged. No wonder I was overcooking things! Now, I only have memories: the scent of flowers, of perfumes, of goodies baking, of air after a summer afternoon rain.

Then came loss of hearing. I found it frustrating and embarrassing having to ask people to repeat themselves, often more than once. I frequently felt alienated. A hearing aid helps, but the loss is permanent. Other losses followed. Injections in an eye every five to six weeks to keep from going blind. COPD making it hard to breathe.

So what do all these challenges have to do with the Center's work and the Touchstones and my journey to being who I'm supposed to be?

EPIPHANY

Recently I had an epiphany about the paradox of life: it is difficult AND it is wonderful. And this journey to become who I'm supposed to be takes a lifetime. I realize that the Touchstones have become part of me. As I continue the journey and face age-related challenges, I can turn to the practices I first learned sitting in circles that the Center convened. I'm not an expert, but I can choose to meet difficulties and loss by offering compassion to myself just as I have to others.

It isn't easy. The losses continue, and I see more ahead. As I write, I'm sitting in my husband's room at a rehabilitation facility, where we just celebrated our 60th wedding anniversary. He has health issues, as do I, but my work at the Center has provided me with the resources and people I need now.

I've had a wonderful, full, happy, and blessed life. I still sit in circles of trust where people speak one at a time, and I can fully participate. With my faith, CRWHE's Touchstones, and the relationships I've made working at the Center, I can prevail.

And in the midst of all the ups and downs, I can say, "At this moment, I am who I am supposed to be."

Earlene Bond is retired and working part-time at Richland College, Thunderwater Organizational Learning Institute (TOLI) and Center for Renewal and Wholeness in Higher Education. She lives in Garland, Texas, with her husband and two dogs. She loves spending time with her family and grandchildren. She can be contacted by email: ebond@dcccd.edu

Becoming Authentic

By Alan Colley

I lived a secret from my eighth year on the planet. That's when I became aware I was not like other boys. I couldn't understand guys who were interested in rough-housing, getting into trouble, and making snide comments about girls, girls who were my friends. At the same time, I was fascinated by them, how they looked and carried themselves so confidently and, in some cases, arrogantly, in my world. I had no word to describe the attraction I had for boys. I was in high school before I had a word for it: "homosexual," a label that I discovered was a curse. Something to be kept secret. Something to be ashamed of. Every attempt I made to come to terms with my sexual orientation was met by denial and warnings by trusted family and friends. Other students bullied me, called me a sissy, and left me out of boy-only activities. I learned secrecy was my future.

In high school, I dated a neighborhood girl who had three brothers. We went to parties and dances but never got past anything other than a light kiss on the cheek. She's the first person who told me she thought I was gay. As many did in my generation, I denied it. And I did that for years, finding sexual liaisons in secret, then feeling guilty. I even got married and had two wonderful children, yet my underlying orientation remained hidden. Well, that's what I told myself.

Of course, keeping a secret like that has consequences. I was chronically plagued by serious health challenges. Their names differed, but the underlying centerpiece was always my fear of being rejected and cast out because I was gay. I began to question whether I was worthy.

"Becoming authentic" seems to me to be a forever journey. Just when I think I have arrived, I have to backtrack and confess I still have a long journey ahead. However, I can point to stages when I actually have stepped up to be more authentic. Even while I say this, one of my "Aha" moments came when I realized that my "authentic" milestones could oh-so-easily become millstones.

REFRAMING MY DILEMMA

A key moment, as I struggled with this dilemma, came in 1988 when I spent a day with a wonderful corporate clinical psychologist who'd been working with me to strengthen my expertise as a work team manager. After an emotional morning, he suggested we take a break and have lunch. As I left his office, he said, "You are one of the most effective managers I work with. I'm not sure there's anything else I can do for you, but I'll see you back here at 2."

I left and walked around town for an hour, too upset to eat. Returning to his office, I broke down in tears and confessed that the biggest burden I carried was being gay. His response was a watershed for me. "Oh, Alan, that's not the biggest burden you carry. The burden you carry is whether you will be authentic in your relationships."

Hearing those words, words I knew were true, completely reframed my dilemma. I realized for the first time that I wasn't a moral failure. I was facing my willingness to be genuine. Sooner or later I was going to have to deal with it, for me, my family, and my career.

The transition was painful and took several more years. In the summer of 1995, I checked myself into a spiritual retreat center to have time alone, away from my family, to deal with this "once and for all." One day, in what I can only describe as deep and yearning prayer, I realized that nothing was wrong with me. There was nothing to fix about my orientation. I just needed to stand up, admit it, come clean with my wife and children, and move on. It was not easy. I hurt the people I loved, not for finally admitting my sexual orientation, but by hiding it for so long. I moved out, divorced, and began the steps to build my life on some level of integrity.

My life opened to possibilities that I never could have conceived. I now believed that since I was being authentic about who I was, life would be smooth sailing! And it was for 10 years. I found the true love of my life, literally falling in love with him within 30 minutes after meeting him. For that I am deeply grateful. Even that milestone, however, was just another way station to being authentic. Let me tell you why.

A KICK IN THE HEAD

I was caught in a place where I was sure I was cool and a master of my life, when a sub-epidural hematoma, a slow leak of blood on my brain, threatened my life. I never considered the possibility of dying, though those around me thought I might. Aside from the medical diagnosis, and months of treatment and recovery, I realized I'd had a serious "kick in the head." I'd been coasting, resting on my self-proclaimed laurels, so to speak, and slowing down. A good friend, a spiritual healer who'd accompanied me through those challenging days, asked: "So you chose to stay and remain among the living. You could have easily opted out. *Why*? What are you going to do by staying here?"

That question, like those earlier words, has remained with me ever since. I felt that I'd not only been given a kick, but also an invitation to do yet another course correction on my journey to authenticity.

As I was recovering from this physical challenge, my friend, Sue Jones, persuaded me to come to Taos, New Mexico, to participate in a week-long workshop designed to prepare facilitators to conduct future Formation retreats. I was still weak and questioned whether I could make it through those demanding days, but I accepted her invitation. From the very first day I was well, hungry, and full of energy. The sense of well-being felt like a miracle to me, an indication that somehow I was on a right path.

During my time in Taos, I elected to participate as a focus person in a circle of trust using the "clearness committee" discernment process with five other trusted people. The experience of openly sharing all my hopes, fears, vulnerabilities and shame was unbelievable because of the unconditional love and support surrounding me.

SANCTUARY

Since then, my life has not been idle. My husband, Dabney, and I have hosted people from around the globe in our home on 160 acres in the middle of the woods in Southwest Oregon. Too often to be random, many of these folks find themselves *called* here, though they didn't sense that until they arrived on the land. The hospitality extended to our guests stems from an awareness I've garnered over the years: that everyone is on a journey toward authenticity. I greet each person with that perspective. I recognize every human is worthy even if he or she doesn't yet see it. Our land is, in my mind, a sanctuary where I have the privilege to hold space for people as they find their own sense of purpose and hear their souls speak.

Am I done with *my* journey of authenticity? Not in the slightest. I keep a daily journal. I am still learning that to be authentic and genuine, I must be willing to acknowledge my admirable and my less-than-stellar character traits; to recognize that I am human after all.

As I look through my entries—even from last week—I am aware I have only begun.

Alan Colley grew up in Ohio, reared his kids in Texas where he also met the love of his life, and now enjoys the life of his dreams in rural Southwest Oregon with his husband, Dabney. He has a (nearly) daily practice of writing in his journal which often surprises him with insights. He and Dabney host people from all over the world on their land, keeping in mind that the space they offer includes holding each guest as worthy of the journey that brought them there. Alan can be reached through his email: ar.colley@gmail.com

No Fear

By Carrole A. Wolin

Away slips a six-figure career once adored.
Crash go investments that once soared.
No fear. My soul cheers.

Away sails a sanctuary once called home.
Sold in record time. Now I venture to parts unknown.
My soul glimmers. No fear.

Love fades away. Grief. Once again
starting over is the plan.
My soul reassures.

When my soul chooses
hope over fear
joy over fear

love and life over fear,
I make peace
with the chaos in this world.

Dr. Carrole A. Wolin is CEO of Coaching Power & StellaLuna Creations, Inc. While she lives in the greater Phoenix metropolitan area with five felines who adopted her, her heart (and sometimes her body) is on Cape Cod and the Outer Banks of North Carolina, the beaches of her wilder days. When she is not dancing or absorbed in hard-covered books, she is checking e-mail from you at drcawolin@gmail.com

It's Your Turn

By Frannie Hill

Eighteen years ago, an encounter with a student named Kelly at Northern Arizona University changed me, my teaching, and the way I listen to and embrace each student's personal story.

Kelly bolted from my classroom in the middle of a lecture. Later she sent me an email to apologize. With her permission, I share what she wrote:

I am so sorry I left your class today and so embarrassed. It takes everything in me to come to your class and today was the hardest. Have you ever felt so alone that you can't breathe at times? Well, that's the story of my life.

Throughout my life, I've become great at putting on a happy face for others, but I'm dying inside. I often think that dying would be better than living because then I could stop acting ... it makes me upset that I even have these thoughts, it just isn't healthy.

My father and I are really, really close, but he doesn't understand why I get sad. He believes that I have everything going for me and that I should be happy all the time. Well, doesn't he know that it isn't that easy? I live alone. I don't really have any friends here, not because I don't want them, it's just that most people already have their friends and there's no room.

I celebrated the anniversary of my sister's death on September 30 and that has me going crazy. You know, that the last thing I ever said to her was: "I wish you were dead," and she died that night.

I have had a good life. I have done things that most people never get to do, and yet I cry at least once a day. I live in my own little world ...

Thanks for listening. Sorry I interrupted class by leaving. I am almost embarrassed to go back.

After reading Kelly's email, a sentence popped into my head. I emailed her back: "Your Past is your REFERENCE Room, not your LIVING Room!"

Since then, I've used that line with other students. I'm continually amazed that when students view the past as a reference point and the living room as where they are now, they discover a brand-new freedom to reinvent themselves.

After hearing many similar stories from students struggling with deep personal issues, I composed a piece entitled *It's Your Turn*. I give it to individual students who've sought me out and hand it out in my classrooms. It's an affirmation which I hope calls forth a sense of self-worth, self-confidence, self-respect and ultimately, self-love. I share it here with you, in the hopes that you will find it of use:

DEAR FRIEND,

Did You Know
That it is Your Turn for:
Joy
Goodness
Enchantment
Gentleness
Laughter
Simplicity
Synchronicity
Your Soul to Find Its Song

Your Turn to:
Rejoice
Smile From The Inside
Celebrate
Know Wonder
Welcome Softness
Restore Hope
Dance Life's Dance
Walk in Beauty's Way

To be Immersed, Enveloped, Surrounded, Hugged, and Inebriated in The Marvelous?

Did You Know

That it's **Okay** *to:*
Let the Pain Trail Away
Erase the Numbness
Allow Healing to Soothe and Comfort
Weep Silently
Receive
Hear Your Own Heart Beat

That it's **Safe** *to:*
Let Go
Not Have to Have Everything Figured Out
Not Have to be Responsible All of the Time
Say "Yes" to Being Alive
Rest: Real Restorative Rest
Listen to Life's Inner Voices

To Look Up to Father Sky in Joyful, Childlike Abandon, Extend Your Arms to the Universe, and Receive Divine Serenity?

Did You Know
That You Can Come Home Again to the Silence
    of Your Own Sacredness
That You Are A Worthy Uncommonly
    Fine Human Being

Full of Miraculous Significance?

Did You Know?

IT'S YOUR TURN!

Frances Ann Hill, Ed. D., is an associate professor at Northern Arizona University's School of Hotel and Restaurant Management. Dr. Hill's teaching and research interests are in the areas of hospitality leadership and ethics, emotional intelligence, interpersonal relationships, and excellence in university teaching. She is an advocate for and practitioner of teaching that touches not only students' minds, but also their hearts. Frannie's interests include mountain biking, river rafting, cross country skiing, hiking, walking, reading, writing, listening to music, and sitting quietly in the forest. Her email is Frances.Hill@nau.edu

Breathing Space

By Loman Clark

What makes a fire burn
is space between the logs,
a breathing space.

Too much of a good thing,
too many logs packed in too tight
can douse the flames
almost as surely
as a pail of water would.

--Judy Sorum Brown, *Fire*

As a boy, I lived in an older home on the edge of the Sonoran Desert. The walls were blocks of rough and variegated natural sandstone. Hues of tan, buff, sand, and taupe were intermixed side-by-side. The house emerged from the landscape, rather than appearing built upon it.

Inside, a fireplace of the same sandstone anchored the living room. On cold winter nights, after everyone else had gone to bed, I enjoyed curling up in the stuffed wing chair nearest the fire. I stared at the glow of hot embers as the fire matured and slowly consumed the wood. In the wee hours of the morning, the contours of the biggest log and its companion kindling sloughed off their sharp edges to settle into piles of grey-white ash. As a child, I didn't know how emblematic my quiet contemplation of the burning logs and the glowing spaces in-between would be of my life.

As years unfolded, milestones collected like a pile of firewood. Educational goals accomplished in K-12, undergraduate, and graduate programs. Time and heart invested in relationships with colleagues, friends, and family members. Homes built, furnished, landscaped, lived in and sold. These aspects of my life had one thing in common: a perpetual placing of the next log on the fire.

But *too much of a good thing, too many logs packed in too tight can douse the flames almost as surely as a pail of water would.*

So it's fortunate that in high school, I developed a distinct personal awareness which began to accompany my perpetual adding of logs. I became conscious of the beauty of creating spaces in between. Along with the rigor of college prep, I signed up for one class period of art each day. No one and nothing else compelled me. Those hours of art were pure pleasure and provided gracious space between expectations and obligations. I knew deep joy.

When it was time to transfer to the university, I interspersed elective studio art classes with the required coursework for a social science degree. The combination prepared me for an opportunity in graduate school. I moved to Berkeley, California, to attend the Graduate Theological Union. GTU was a consortium of nine schools of theology, education, worship arts and pastoral care. I chose the Franciscan School of Theology for a study of prayer and meditation.

Day one began unremarkably. We entered a standard classroom, configured with modular all-in-one chairs and desktops. Everything in the room faced forward. When a priest entered the room to guide us, he quietly moved a sliding panel to reveal a chalkboard with the phrase: "*Shri Ram, JayRam, JayJayRamon.*"

The chant was our first shared activity. In rough translation, the Sanskrit words convey devotion to God and solicitation for a pure heart. To get us started, the priest sang through the words and the corresponding notes. After he repeated the phrase several times, we tentatively joined him. At first, we were distracted. On the periphery, each of us had a view of someone else in the room. Many of us also had to look past the back of a classmate's head in front of us to view the words. We were sensitized and highly conscious of each other's presence.

With repetition, the phrase and the notes gained familiarity. As we became more comfortable, we closed our eyes. The focus became the sound we made as we sang the notes in unison. As our breathing began to synchronize, the initial awkwardness subsided. Any one of us could feel free to pause, take a catchup breath, swallow or adjust our posture for comfort. When we started, there may have been apprehension of our individual singing voices being exposed, but hesitancy gave way to a collective sound that filled our ears, our heads, and the room. Soon everything in the room began to vibrate with the frequency of each note.

The priest led us into deepening the practice. We shifted from singing to humming. The sense of unity continued without words, based upon the shared notes, pacing, and breathing. A bell-like resonance originated from all around us and permeated us. The effect was eerie, as if the walls had disappeared. There was a profound sense of oneness as we continued for several minutes.

The final level of practice was to sit together in stilled silence. When the words and music fell away, our experience of connection continued in the void. Gone were thoughts of assignments for other classes. Absent was any thought of what we'd previously eaten or would eat next. Everything was stripped away other than practicing presence together.

Without knowing it, I had experienced a foretaste of my future, a way to put into practice the long-ago lesson from the fire, attention to spaces between the logs. The impact of that first day of class remained with me. Years later, my love of creativity and reflective practices combined to ignite my studies in counseling psychology, personal and employee development, wellness and a return to art. As a helping professional at a community college, I supported the lives of aspiring youth as well as adults who wanted to resume their dreams or get a fresh start. And the lessons continued as I fostered space in the busy lives of those I nurtured: to pause, to take stock, to transform, and to serve.

Beginning in the 2000's, friends from the Center for Renewal and Wholeness in Higher Education reminded me once again of the lessons learned while meditating by the fire. Thank you: Ann, Sue, Elaine, Yolanda, Guy, Steve, Bill, Debra, Garth, Earlene and cherished colleagues. Also, I might not have found my way, except for the kindness and collegiality of Maricopa Community Colleges compadres: Betsy, Donna, and Paul, followed by Corina, Anna, and Maria.

What's next as I plan retirement? My core practices of creating art and meditating continue to enliven me. They are both muse and lover. They create breathing spaces in which I can honor and tend my fire for many years to come; in which, as Judy Brown says in her poem *Fire*, "*the flame that knows just how it wants to burn can find its way.*"

What makes a fire burn
is space between the logs,
a breathing space.

Too much of a good thing,
too many logs packed in too tight
can douse the flames
almost as surely

as a pail of water would.

So building fires
requires attention
to the spaces in between,
as much as to the wood.

When we are able to build
open spaces
in the same way
we have learned
to pile on the logs,
then we can come to see how
it is fuel, and the absence of fuel
together, that make fire possible.

We only need to lay a log
lightly from time to time.
A fire
grows
simply because the space is there,
with openings
in which the flame
that knows just how it wants to burn
can find its way.

--Judy Sorum Brown

Loman Clark has resided in metro Phoenix for over half a century. The seasons of his life he celebrates by recalling the names and faces of those with whom life has been shared, whether human or critter. Today he shares his home with Francisco, Chuey & Lulu. Loman may be contacted at phoenixfireflight@yahoo.com

Connecting Myself to My Self

By Lisa Davis

The unexpected. An opportunity. A chance encounter.

Each can be a mere event, unnoticed or quickly forgotten, or they can connect in such a way that they become a catalyst for something more.

Three such seemingly disparate experiences shaped my story.

Until this series of events, I did mostly as expected, as I was told - without much thought. I met the milestones of success professionally and personally. But, as T. S. Eliot pointed out in *Four Quartets*, I had missed the meaning:

> *We had the experience but missed the meaning,*
> *And approach to the meaning restores the experience*
> *In a different form, beyond any meaning*
> *We can assign to happiness.*

Then these events happened in quick succession, helping me claim the story as my own, helping to restore the meaning, to connect myself to my Self. Until then, my experience was inauthentic and frankly uncontemplated, directed by expectations rather than deep desire or a deep sense of self.

A mere three events: a diagnosis, a formation experience, a chance encounter on a plane.

A DIAGNOSIS

A few years ago, a diagnosis changed my story profoundly and totally unexpectedly. I had been a nurse and worked in a variety of health care settings, helping others adjust to their "new normal" after devastating disease or debilitating illness. I was told I was good at it and should teach it, so I became a university professor.

After a routine health care visit, my health care provider suggested I get a renal ultrasound to check renal profusion after taking certain medications for several years. That sounded reasonable, so I had the test and thought no more about it until I got the call.

"You have kidney cancer," the nurse reported in a message left on my office phone. That was it. Cancer? What? It was 4:30 pm on a Friday so when I called back I could only get the answering machine, into which I just blubbered. What do I do?

I went home and spent the weekend planning for death—putting insurance paperwork into one pile, things to toss in piles, things to donate in piles, thoughts in piles. I walked around my home as if in a fog, moving in slow motion. What does this mean? How long do I have?

Returning to work on Monday was surreal, excruciatingly so. Friendly students, faculty and staff greeted me with the standard "Hi, how are you?"

How am I? I had never been so struck by the greeting—never really paid attention to the words of a simple greeting. But I did now. Each well-meaning greeting opened a new wound, reminding me of my diagnosis.

How do I answer that? How am I?

After that hopeless, helpless weekend and suffering through many Monday greetings of "How are you," plans for treatment began to take shape, and my story morphed to that of someone who had hope, but hope for what? The line from Mary Oliver's poem, *The Summer Day*, played over and over in my mind:

> **What is it you plan to do**
> **with your one wild and precious life?**

After surgery and through an extended recovery, that thought continued: "What would I do with my wild and precious life?" The previous year, I had attended CRWHE facilitation training in Taos, New Mexico, and now it became clear: I must go back to Taos. Taos became a talisman, but that year's training was to start in just a few weeks. I contacted CRWHE and was graciously told, "Come."

A FORMATION EXPERIENCE

I wish I could say I lived divided no more from that point, but one of the things I learned is that it's all about the journey.

The journey in Taos allowed me to ground myself in my new normal; Clearness Committee affirmed that I was allowing too much of my story to be written by others, not myself—my wild and precious self. The Taos formation experience also gave me a voice. I discovered that while I may not be able to verbalize my innermost thoughts, I could *write* them. I could put truth to paper that I couldn't say out loud. That was a step in a positive direction for me.

I love serendipity. In the gift shop at the Mable Dodge Luhan House (the site of the formation training), I found *The Essential Writer's Notebook: A Step–by–Step Guide to Better Writing* by Natalie Goldberg. In it she admonishes us to keep our hand moving, to trust ourselves, to "meet our own gritty mind," and to tell the truth. For me, this was remarkable: not that I didn't know this intellectually already, but that I could and would do it. Needless to say, I got the book.

Rather than see myself mainly through the lenses of others, I was able, through writing, to shift my gaze inward, to how I was in the world and how the world was in me. Writing expanded me.

I had seen this same book there the year before, but I was a different person then. Now, everything was in stereo. I was previously consumed with doing—doing teaching, doing research, doing what was expected of a college professor, of a mother, of a citizen. While I knew intellectually the importance of being—being with, being authentic, being human, being present—it was not a consistent part of my story. I was beginning to discover *being* more clearly.

I remembered seeing a visual of the ocean years ago when nurse theorist, Margaret Newman, described health as expanding consciousness at the International Association of Human Caring Annual Conference in Montreal, Canada. She said that if you are a wave in the ocean, you exist as a wave but you are affected by the waves around you, by the moon, by wind and weather—constantly changing but still the same. Further, to understand that pattern, one must know the story. My story could be affected by what happens to me or what others tell me, but my story (my little wave in the ocean) was in how I reacted to these waves around me.

Wow! My story was told by me in terms of how I *reacted* to the events around and within me.

Subsequently, I engaged in mindfulness practices to become more present-oriented. Writing became a means to that end, helping me to notice more of being in the world, helping me to reflect: I was, I will be, but most important, I am.

A CHANCE ENCOUNTER

Shortly after I started writing in earnest, I had another chance encounter that proved to be a profound experience.

On a plane to New York, I sat in the back in an aisle seat. One seat in front of me and to the left sat a manic rabbi—manic in the excited, energetic sense, not the pathological sense. He was rail thin and wore a black yarmulke; a *tallit katan* was visible at his waist. He had a thin, open face with deep dimples and bright brown eyes behind octagonal glasses. But most striking was his perpetual motion and deep need to talk (something I assiduously avoid on a plane, normally).

He first engaged the woman in the seat in front of me. "What makes you happy? What do you want most in life?" He was not making small talk; he showed a genuine interest in hearing the answers.

"God wants us to be happy," he stated while gesticulating wildly. "He wants us to have options. There can be no choice of love without the option of no love. If there is no choice, it is not love but fear."

He was young, perhaps early 30's and unmarried. He told those of us listening that he had been at the Pentagon exploring the option of becoming a Navy chaplain. He went on to ask about faith and faith beliefs—not to question, but to understand. He seemed to have a need to understand.

He said choice equals love, that it is an expression of free will. In this entire dialogue he was in constant motion—hand gestures, torso, even his speech was fast and clipped as if the words take too long to say. I imagined his brain working, neurons flashing and firing in a display like Fourth-of-July fireworks.

Free will. Despite his distracting movement, I was enthralled by his thoughts. His next statement dumbfounded me: "I am not religious because it is so limiting."

How incongruous this seemed to me in my understanding of the term; for me, he epitomized being religious. I have since come to understand that in Judaism, religion is to know the answers, whereas secularism is to seek the questions. My mind wraps around this understanding as I reflect back on his words: "I am not religious because it is so limiting. I want to be happy. If I am happy, God is happy. What makes me happy brings me closer to God."

As we neared landing, his face looked quizzical and he pulled out a white legal pad and pen and wrote. He was inside himself now and was still. For the first time his frenzied movement quieted as he took his pen in his left hand and thoughtfully and deliberately wrote.

Questions. It was about questions, not answers.

He stimulated questions in all those around him, certainly in me. As the plane pulled into the gate, he popped—yes popped!— up from his seat and hurried down the aisle. A rabbi, a teacher of questions.

THREE BECAME ONE

A diagnosis, a formation experience, and a chance encounter on a plane. Three experiences became one which now has profound meaning, a connection of myself to my Self and to the Universe; a direction for the experience of life.

Each moment has meaning, my voice is my own, and my role is to embrace the moments fully, to reflect, and to ask questions. T. S. Eliot continues to speak to me from the *Four Quartets*:

> *For most of us, there is only the unattended*
> *Moment, the moment in and out of time,*
> *The distraction fit, lost in a shaft of sunlight,*
> *The wild thyme unseen, or the winter lightning*
> *Or the waterfall, or music heard so deeply*
> *That it is not heard at all.*

Dr. Lisa Davis is a recently retired Professor of Nursing, West Texas A&M University. Currently she resides in Winston Salem, North Carolina where she enjoys the beautiful countryside, reading, writing, quilting, and forever learning. She can be reached at lisaadavis30@gmail.com

Writing from the Heart:
An Invitation

By Joyce Boatright

The process for change is filled with conflict and chaos. Writing from my heart rather than my head helps me navigate the path to wholeness.

I have spent a major portion of my adult life reflecting, refocusing, and renewing my personal goal to live an undivided life. As a devotee of the work of the CRWHE and Parker Palmer, I practice the principles of authenticity, always seeking progress rather than perfection.

Becoming a credible facilitator would be impossible without personally immersing myself in this work. I am both a writer and a teacher of writing, and this is what I know is true: Writing is thinking on paper.

Natalie Goldberg, author and Zen practitioner, encourages us to write fast so we can write ahead of our internal critic. When I follow her advice, I discover what I honestly believe about a topic or issue. I write about paradoxes in my professional and personal life so I can hold the creative tension and be willing to ask the questions, knowing they, rather than the answers, guide me in a life that matters.

After 49 years of teaching, the last 25 at Lone Star College-North Harris, I continue, post retirement, my life's vocation by facilitating writing workshops at the Houston Jung Center.

In these classes, I create the space for adults to explore their fears (both real and imagined) that keep them from living fully. I believe each of us is the story we tell ourselves, and if we don't like our story, we can change the story and rediscover our authentic selves.

I teach the craft and creativity of writing deeply, and I use my heart's ear to listen to participants' life stories. I guide people, through writing, to heal their psychological wounds and grow fully into their authentic selves. I support my participants as they tap into the fierce courage needed to move toward their destiny as whole, creative individuals. My greatest honor is bearing witness to this process. In a circle of trust, each writing group embraces the preciousness of deep listening as each participant gives voice to his or her individual narrative.

I invite you to explore similar questions to those in our writing circles of trust: What are your heart's desires? What propels you toward them? What diverts you from them?

I invite you to write from your heart.

Joyce Boatright, EdD, is a teacher, writer, and storyteller. Retired in 2016 from Lone Star College System, she facilitates life-writing workshops for self-awareness and personal development at the Carl G. Jung Center in Houston, TX. She can be reached through email: btrght@gmail.com

Freedom

By RubyRenee Wood

If I could choose
I'd have rain everyday
And that rain
Would be cool and biting
Certainly never warmer than
The sweetest fall night

Then I'd stand naked outside
Until I was drenched and shivering
My neighbors aghast

But then maybe
My better choice is
The rain turning to sleet

With tiny ice needles
Stabbing and slicing
My skin so cold
That the ice bounces away
All my neighbors disgusted
But not surprised

Or if I could really have my wish
There'd be a hail storm
Dropping directly overhead
With hail the size of
Boulders

I'd curve my arms
Above my head
Like a womb
My fingers cupped together
Ready to receive

Then each giant hailstone
Would magically pause
At my feather soft fingertips
And explode

My neighbors, marveling
At the sparkling ice shards spiraling down
Failing to notice
That I'd melted into water
And was floating away
Woman liquefied

Although I think I'd like to keep my nipples
So, I'd be this six foot long river
With a pair of nipples bobbing along
The neighbors whipping out their recording devices

And what would be delirious
Would be to wake up as the water
In somebody's drinking glass
Minus the nipples of course
Filtered out
At the water treatment plant
But presumably
The flavor still there

RubyRenee Wood supports the arts as an Office Assistant to the Carlsen Center Performing Arts Series General Manager at Johnson County Community College. She lives in Kansas City, Missouri, where she pursues any and every type of creative expression with her darling husband CHVCK and cat Blanche. She can be contacted through e-mail: RubyRenee44@gmail.com

Finding the Stranger Who Is My Self

By Julie Moore-Felux

How does one find and stay connected to one's purpose in life? This is a central question those who engage in Courage work, as participants and as facilitators, ask themselves.

In some people's lives, getting clear about purpose comes as an epiphanic experience, a sudden recognition of what one is intended to do. For example, I have a friend who was driving down the highway when she was overwhelmed by a voice, not her own, that told her to buy a farm and begin raising miniature horses. Today, she runs an organization that uses miniature horses to promote literacy and to provide outreach to children and adults experiencing transition, trauma and grief. She is clear she is living out her calling.

I also met a woman who told me about hiking in the forest when she experienced a visceral awakening. She returned home, quit a highly competitive job, and became a chaplain. Today she works in a hospital, comforting patients and their families, work she is "meant to do."

I've had moments of clarity—sitting in a circle during a retreat, during Quaker meeting when I was compelled to rise and speak, and while walking in nature and soul-soaking gratitude flooded me. But none of these moments carried with them a sudden and undeniable awakening to my purpose in life, what I was meant to do.

When I think about the events which led me to the work I do now as an educator and a Renewal and Wholeness facilitator, I can only explain them as a series of choices that allowed me to return to and to stay connected to myself. And I have experienced my sense of self as something I was always giving away.

The youngest of four, I was born nearly 10 years after the last of my three siblings. During my elementary school years, we moved many times due to my father's career. As a result, I attended seven different elementary schools, four of which were in Germany.

I remember the mixture of dread and hopefulness that accompanied me each time I entered a new classroom. *Would the other kids be nice to me? Would they want to be friends? Would I be able to catch up with the work they were doing?* The teacher would say, "Class, we have a new student today, please say hello to Julie." I could feel their eyes sizing me up in the silent appraising air of little children. The verdict would come later on the playground.

LISTENING TO MY VOICE

During those years, I developed the ability to remain self-contained and learned to listen to my own inner voice. Because I was a good listener, I learned a great deal about people, the differences that set them apart and the ways they were so much the same. Outside of school, I was often in the company of adults, frequently participating in their conversations. I read voraciously and loved the feeling of slipping into the different worlds that opened up between the covers of books.

The gift of these childhood experiences was a paradox. I was both self-conscious and aware of my consciousness, introspective and outgoing, talkative and a good listener, a friend and a stranger. These elements of both/and were useful in many subsequent relationships. For better or worse, people wanted to open up to me, share their worries, and ask me for my insight, perhaps because I gave attention without expecting it in return. This shoulder-lending, problem-solving capacity led me to friendships with people, quite often many years my senior. On more than one occasion I have had someone tell me, "I can't believe I am telling you all of this, you are just a kid," or "We've only just met, but here I am telling you my life story." In my own family, I became the counselor, the one who got the phone call when there was an emotional crisis, the one who was asked to fix things.

As I tried to care for others, I did not share my worries, fears, or troubles. I did not tell my story. I gave my attention, my time, myself. I didn't believe I could ask for those things in return. I took care of myself . . . and in the process, I got lost in the various roles and responsibilities of my life. I found that although there were many people whom I cared for, and who relied on me, I often felt alone and isolated.

SHAKING UP MY LIFE

Then a sequence of events shook my life. After 14 years in an unhealthy marriage, I finally found the courage to divorce. There were times when I doubted myself. Wasn't marriage supposed to involve sacrifice? Was I being selfish? It took several months to reconcile my fear of being the agent of despair for my family and the realization that I had given too much away for too long.

Once I ended the marriage, I had to re-examine my ideas about healthy relationships. I wasn't sure if I would find another partner, but love found me. I met Thomas and for the first time entered a relationship based on trust, mutual respect, and deep admiration. I experienced the thrill of a new romance, but mostly, I was surprised by the genuine sense of peace I felt with him. Thomas lived in his own skin, with integrity and authenticity, and accepted me unconditionally. As our relationship deepened, the words of the mystic poet Rumi-

Your task is not to seek for love, but merely to seek and find all the barriers within yourself that you have built against it. resonated inside me. I found a new kind of courage; I began to believe I could be vulnerable again.

About 10 months later, my newfound openness to vulnerability was put to the test. I was 40 years old, with two kids, a rewarding career, wonderful friends and the love of my life. I thought my future was limitless; then cancer ambushed me. Within three months of finding a lump in my breast, I had a bilateral mastectomy, reconstruction, and started chemotherapy and radiation.

Cancer carried me all the way to the edge of a cliff, dismantling many barriers I'd relied on for protection. I had to learn to accept help. While I lay on the couch, my co-workers, neighbors, friends, and family rallied. There was a daily delivery of meals for months. Cards, letters and gifts, even from people I knew only in passing, flooded my home. My best friend held my hand while Thomas shaved my head. Two weeks later, Thomas proposed. One night shortly after we became engaged, I asked him if he was sure about taking this step; didn't he want to wait and see if I would make it through this fight. He held me in his arms and in a voice choked with tears said, "I want to be married to you, whether it's for two weeks or forever."

In many ways, my illness allowed me to recognize the best in others and in myself, but as with all things, light does not exist without shadow. When I became ill, all I could do was ride the wave of each treatment; I no longer had the energy to push my demons down. The combination of physical exhaustion, medication, and treatment-induced depression allowed feelings of sadness, anger, and disappointment I'd spent years storing away in my soul's basement to rise. I no longer tolerated pettiness, insincerity, and BS. Some of my relationships shifted.

I began to learn the difference between putting up walls and establishing boundaries. Once again, paradox manifest in my life. Cancer allowed me to experience radical love, profound kindness, and generosity. It also revealed difficult truths and carried me to some of the darkest corners of my consciousness.

When the aftershocks of what felt like an earthquake subsided and the dust began to settle, I realized things were going to have to be different. There were some cracks and fissures in the way I thought about myself, and I wasn't quite sure how I was going to navigate this new terrain. A path forward opened up about a year later when a colleague of mine invited me to a formation retreat for faculty at our college.

"I think this is something you need," she said, "and you're the kind of person who will connect with this experience." Little did I know at the time, she was naming one of my birthright gifts.

At the retreat, we sat in a circle, spent time journaling, observed silence, and extended to one another the gift of deep listening. Since I'd attended Quaker meetings, the format was somewhat familiar; but instead of practicing stillness to hear God, we listened to our authentic selves and reflected upon our life's purpose. A year later, I was invited to apply to train as a facilitator.

At some point during that year, I encountered Derek Walcott's *Love After Love*. These lines speak beautifully about what it is like to come home to who you are:

> **Give back your heart**
> **to itself, to the stranger who has loved you**
>
> **all your life, whom you ignored**
> **for another, who knows you by heart.**

Through formation work, I have given back my heart to the stranger who has loved me all my life. I now know how to give without giving myself away. I've also faced and embraced my shadow side. I still stumble into the well-worn tracks of old habits and sometimes have to put my ego in time-out. My call came not through an epiphany or a sudden burst of awareness but by learning to listen to that voice that has always lived inside of me, the one that welcomes me home to my own heart.

Julie Moore-Felux is an Associate Professor of English at Northwest Vista College. She hold an M.A. in English from the University of Texas at San Antonio and a PhD in Curriculum and Instruction from New Mexico State University. Julie lives in San Antonio, Texas with her husband Thomas and is a proud mom to Julienne and Alec. She has a wicked sense of humor, cries easily and without embarrassment at the movies, loves wholeheartedly, and always tells it like it is. Julie can be reached at jmoore-felux@alamo.edu

Following the Invitations of Spirit, Living into an Undivided Life

By T. S. Pennington

2001 was the year my life took a dramatic change in direction.

Of course, like most Americans, I was deeply saddened and stressed by the attacks on the World Trade Towers and the ensuing Gulf War. But it was a personal experience that redirected my life.

When I tell people the story of how my life changed, I first mention that March of that year I was told that I needed the equivalent of quintuple heart bypass surgery. I had the surgery just after the end of the school year.

Before the surgery, I was asked to write a vision of how I imagined my life would be in 10 years. The idea was to give me something to look forward to, a reason to want to recover and thrive. My vison of this future was basically a continuation of the life I was enjoying at that time. I wrote that I would continue to teach full-time until 2011 and then part-time in my retirement. That I would still be living in the Kansas City area and caring for my aging mother, if she were still alive. And that I would continue to attend the annual meeting of the SIGCSE (Special Interest Group Computer Science Educators) of the Association for Computing Machinery and perhaps write a programming textbook. Teaching programming was my passion.

But then in August my spirit accepted an invitation that sent me re-exploring paths that I had walked away from in the late 70's.

The weekend before the start of fall classes, my school district offered a Formation Sampler Retreat, grounded in the writing of Dr. Parker J. Palmer and facilitated by Dr. Sally Z. Hare. The Metropolitan Community Colleges of Kansas City (MCCKC) had already invited Palmer to keynote our annual district-wide meeting. I remember being intrigued by the challenge of bringing spirituality into public education without violating the separation of church and state. I read a couple of Palmer's articles on teaching being a vocation, a calling. His writing resonated with my love of being an educator and my joy in sharing that passion with other teachers from across the district and from a variety of disciplines.

The retreat, with about 30 of us in the circle, fanned the ember of my dormant spirit into a flame. Hare shared the Touchstones, which gave me a sense of safety. I loved the use of poems as focus points for our reflections. As the retreat ended, Hare invited us to be a part of a seasonal series of eight retreats over the next two years. My spirit has always been deeply intertwined with nature, so the idea of using the seasons as a way of exploring spirituality was an invitation I could not refuse.

Kathy Kiser, a fellow teacher from my campus, said there was a plan to get the district to fund a team to go through the CRWHE formation facilitator training. I immediately volunteered. We started our training in Fall 2001, when the Center for Renewal and Wholeness in Higher Education (CRWHE) was still the Center for Formation in the Community College (CFCC).

POETRY AND RUMI AND ANDREW HARVEY

Poems were the primary things used in the facilitator training and at our MCCKC retreats. I had forgotten how much I had enjoyed poetry when I was in my early twenties. Some of the most meaningful poems for me were by Jalal ad-Din Rumi. I enjoyed his deep devotion to the Beloved, that he embraced multiple traditions and his mysticism. I started collecting books of poetry, especially translations of Rumi's poems. Andrew Harvey became my favorite translator of Sufi poetry, and when I read his autobiographical books, I decided that I needed to meet him in person.

Following my soul's longing, I attended a retreat with Harvey the following spring in Fork of Ivy, North Carolina. I related to Andrew because he was like me, a gay man and a mystic who honored all faiths. I was even more impressed with Andrew in person and continued to attend many events with him. It was also at this retreat that I fell in love with the Blue Ridge Mountains. I decided that if I got a chance to retire there, I would.

Andrew Harvey spoke highly of writers who inspired him, one of whom was Matthew Fox, who had established a new pedagogy for learning spirituality that melded the ancient Western wisdom tradition with contemporary scientists and modern mystics. Fox was an early and influential exponent of a movement that came to be known as Creation Spirituality and created the University of Creation Spirituality. Fox had been excommunicated from the Catholic Church because of his views, and I felt empathy for Fox because when I was 20, I was told that the Jesuit seminary would not accept me because I was reading Pierre Teilhard de Chardin, who wrote that evolution was God's method of creation. De Chardin was silenced by the Catholic Church; none of his books was published during his lifetime.

Attending a conference in San Francisco in the spring of 2004, I decided to take a break to explore Fox's University of Creation Spirituality in Oakland. Walking up the stairs past a mural that showed the evolution of the Universe and life on Earth made me know that I was among people who loved creation as much I did.

I applied to the University of Creation Spirituality before I left that day.

By the time I attended the SIGCSE conference in February of 2005, I realized that my passion for teaching computer science was gone. I retired in May, so that I would have more time to care for my mother. But since I had lost my passion, it was an easy adjustment. I only taught for two years after my retirement.

I was unable to travel out of town to attend classes at the university for most of 2005 and all of 2006 because of my mother's failing health. I needed another way to feed my spirit. It was then that the Universe sent me another invitation. I happened to see a small ad in *Ode* magazine for One Spirit Interfaith Seminary in New York City. I went online and downloaded a pamphlet about their program. Its director, Rev. Diane Berke, wrote in a way that directly connected to my heart and spirit.

I applied to the program and was accepted in the fall of 2006. During the first several months I attended the classes online. The first time I attended in person was in March of 2007 for an Easter weekend retreat with Andrew Harvey. In his teachings and especially his book, *The Hope: A Guide to Sacred Activism*, he encouraged persons to discover what breaks their hearts the most and then to use their talents and gifts towards healing that wound. At the end of the first day of the Easter retreat, Andrew asked us to spend one hour that evening writing down all the things about the world that broke our hearts.

It was one of the most painful nights of my life.

FINDING MY GREATEST HEARTBREAK

A couple of months after the Easter retreat, in a class on creativity with Angeles Arrien, another student in the class mirrored back to me that I had expressed great sorrow that the people of various religious traditions would use that as a basis to hurt and even kill people of other traditions. I had found my greatest heartbreak and now I needed to find a way of healing.

In the summer of 2007, I attended a retreat for One Spirit first-year students. Rev. Berke spoke about Interspirituality and Brother Wayne Teasdale. Reading Teasdale's book *The Mystic Heart: Discovering a Universal Spirituality in the World's Religions* gave me insight about how to heal my greatest heartbreak.

I felt *The Mystic Heart* was addressing the conflict between traditions, just as I felt Palmer's book *Healing the Heart of Democracy: The Courage to Create Politics Worthy of the Human Spirit* was doing for our political situation. Brother Wayne was one of the two co-chairs for the second Parliament of the World's Religions, held in Chicago on the 100th anniversary of the first parliament. He encouraged people to become mystics in their tradition, even if they had no formal tradition, and then to explore what they had in common and what the traditions could learn from each other. He had a vision of an organization where the mystics of all traditions and those without a tradition could come together. He called it the Universal Order of Sannyasa, but sadly, he passed away in 2004, before he could create his vision. In reading Brother Teasdale, the flame of my spirit had become a bonfire. I knew to the core of my being that spirituality was the foundation of all faiths, that it permeated all belief systems and transcended them.

I returned to One Spirit to ask Rev. Berke to be my dissertation advisor. She said no, but knowing that I was hoping to base my dissertation on Brother Teasdale's ideas and James W. Fowler's *Stages of Faith*, she suggested that I talk to Dr. Kurt Johnson, who happened to be there at that moment. In fact, as spirit would have it, we had ridden up in the elevator together that morning. Johnson was a very close friend of Brother Wayne and was working diligently to keep his vision alive; he wanted to create the Universal Order of Sannyasa to honor Brother Wayne. In late 2008, he invited me and several others to work with him to fulfill this dream; on January 9, 2010, the Universal Order was created at a church in Washington, D.C. Because Sannyasa is sacred in the Hindu tradition, it was decided to rename this order as the *Community of the Mystic Heart*. I served on its leadership circle for the next four years, helped draft several of its statements, and I read early versions and made suggestions for Johnson's book *The Coming Interspiritual Age*, which was published in 2012. In the last two years, I have moved away from this community.

INTERFAITH MINISTER

I was ordained an interfaith minister in 2008. I never envisioned myself doing typical duties of a minister such as performing weddings, baby blessings, funeral services or leading a church. I went through the One Spirit program so that I would have a solid knowledge base of the world's religions. I used this foundation to first work with the Greater Kansas City Interfaith Council and then with the Mountain Area Interfaith forum and to teach religion courses at the Osher Lifelong Learning Institute (OLLI) at the University of North Carolina-Asheville.

My training as a CRWHE facilitator served me well as I facilitated multiple sections of a course based on James W. Fowler's *Stages of Faith: The Psychology of Human Development and the Quest for Meaning*. I conducted the class as a dialogue group rather than a traditional lecture class. I used the Touchstones to create a safe space for all of us to speak about how we lived our spirituality. As in the circles of trust, I was awed by the variety and scope of the stories that emerged from the OLLI students as they shared their stories.

SEEING THE PATTERNS

As I reflected on all those stories, I realized that patterns emerged, which formed the ways I now view universal spirituality. But these patterns felt fragmented until I read Charles Eisenstein's *The More Beautiful World Our Hearts Know is Possible*. I then understood the power of stories that we are told by others and the versions of those stories we tell ourselves. I agree with Eisenstein that human beings live out of stories, mostly stories of separation. He advocates that we need to move away from those stories to ones of interconnection and interdependency. Eisenstein is asking his readers to live an undivided life; I want to do the same.

When I began this journey, I agreed with Parker Palmer that the soul was a shy animal that would not come into a forest clearing unless it felt safe. But now I know that my soul has evolved to be a beast, who will not let me alone, who demands that its voice be heard. I am informed by all the writers I have read and teachers I have been with, but it is the intuition of my spirit which is now the main source of my inspiration.

My current work is the development of my *Framework*, a map of the stories of relationships that all of us have as human beings. It contains five areas: Creativity, Mystery, Cosmos & Nature, People and Oneself. Each of the areas contains more specific aspects as I work to include as many different relationships as possible.

I have also incorporated from Ken Wilber's audio program, *The One, Two, Three of God*. Wilbur refers to the human way of viewing perspectives of either the third, the second or the first person: that if we think of anything in the third person, then we either ignore it or treat it as an object. When we move to second person (an I and Thou), then we must interact with it either in a positive or negative manner. If we think of something in the first person, then we identify with it. In this context, I understand that Eisenstein is asking all of us to move consciously from a third person perspective into second person with as many concepts, communities, people, nature and fragmentated parts of ourselves as we possibly can. I ask my readers to contemplate in which perspective they approach each aspect of the five areas of the *Framework*.

I know this work is greater than I can accomplish by myself. I continue to be guided by my spirit and to look for colleagues. From sitting in numerous Circles of Trust, I have learned that humanity will never have one story that everyone will claim as their truth. If we can speak our truth knowing that it belongs to just us and hold the truth of others with an open mind and a loving heart, then we will be living an undivided life. Just as the Earth's diversity of life forms and natural environments gives human beings a profound sense of awe and beauty, so should the diversity of the human story.

I encourage you to let your shy soul mature into a beast. Can you imagine the new animal kingdom we might create together?

T. S. Pennington is a retired instructor of computer science from the Metropolitan Community Colleges of Kansas City and an ordained interfaith minister. He lives in the Blue Ridge Mountains, just outside of Asheville, North Carolina, with his two Siamese cats, Buddha and Bodhi. He can be reached through his website AllOurRelationships.org

Paradox!

By Glenda S. Williams

Creates understanding
Makes life less demanding

Turns white into black
Turns black into white
Tumbles the space
Between shadow and light

Paradox!

Let's you be you
And me be me
I speak my truth individually
We speak our truth collectively
We speak our truth in community

Paradox!

Bound and unbound
Silence and sound

Don't make no suggestions
I'm living the questions

Paradox!

Forget either/or
I don't know what that's for
In the middle I stand
In the peace of both/and

Centered I stand
In the peace of both/and

Dr. Glenda Williams, Psychology Professor at Lone Star College, is passionate about teaching, learning, and facilitating Circles of Trust. She lives in Spring, Texas, with her husband David and springer spaniel Bella. Glenda loves to golf, travel, read, and ride her motorcycle. She can be contacted at glenda.williams@lonestar.edu

Learning to Live an Undivided Life

By Kristina Lizardy-Hajbi

My love of learning has been a significant part of what makes me *me*.

One of my earliest memories is of Dad waking me each morning and going through the Sesame Street alphabet flashcards. He would gently nudge me awake from my slumber and whisper, "It's time to learn."

Groggy-eyed, I'd sit up slowly and he'd settle at the edge of the bed for my daily lesson. This was one of my favorite times of the day and became a regular routine until I was able to identify each letter with ease.

In my toddler years, I thumbed through my Disney read-along books while listening to accompanying cassette tapes until I wore them out. In a favorite "big kid" book—one with lots of words I couldn't yet read—there was a picture of a girl doing homework. I spent hours studying that picture, dreaming of the day when I too would have homework.

On my very first day of school, I was so excited about being in a classroom that I couldn't understand why some of my soon-to-be friends were crying and begging to go home. For me, there was no sadness or tears when it came to learning!

This desire for knowledge has looped itself through my life like a sturdy vine. Another vine, faith, nurtured by adults who served as beloved spiritual mentors, wound itself within my very being. As a child, I encountered the presence of God outwardly through regular church attendance, Sunday School, Bible camps, and private religious schools. I also encountered God inwardly through prayers, dreams, readings, and other experiences that I can only describe as mysterious and wonder-filled.

Even as a young adult, I felt "called" by an energy gently guiding me toward an exploration of what lay below the surface of the everyday, or perhaps was intertwined within the everyday itself. This nudging asked me to pay attention to what was sacred in humanity and creation and to walk alongside others also seeking to catch a glimpse of the holy.

KNOWLEDGE AND FAITH

The combined desire for knowledge and a strong faith set me on a journey which led to my current vocation as a United Church of Christ Minister and a faculty member and administrator at a United Methodist seminary. Not just any seminary, but the place in which my own training as a minister occurred!

As an undergrad, I felt an inner nudging to consider ministry as a vocational path. My sense of calling was confirmed by friends and mentors, so after graduation, I began serving as staff at a small, urban multiracial/multilingual congregation in Denver, Colorado.

Very quickly, my 21-year-old self was overwhelmed. I realized my experience as a campus fellowship leader had not prepared me for what I was experiencing in this church, and I needed additional training. I enrolled in the closest seminary, Iliff School of Theology, which began a time of holistic learning, skill development, spiritual formation, and openings to new possibilities of faith.

In spiritual direction sessions, ongoing conversations with mentors, and at a week-long silent retreat, the way forward became clear. My call was to mentor, teach, equip church leaders, and support others on their spiritual journeys, to live and work in a setting where the vines of knowledge and faith flourished. I had a deep desire to shape environments in which others could nurture their spirituality and capacities for ministry. My role at the seminary—teaching and designing curricula for the professional formation of ministry, theology, and social justice students—is one in which all of my gifts and passions can be shared and stretched in new ways.

SOUL AND ROLE

In my early days as a minister, I thought the very nature of my work would create an automatic connection between "soul and role." Today, as I provide students with opportunities to engage more deeply, I find it's not any easier for me to live what Parker Palmer terms "an undivided life" than those I serve. Perhaps that's why I'm so drawn to spiritual practices and inner work—I need and am renewed by the gifts they offer as much as anyone else.

Over the years of ministering and teaching, my sense of holy has extended into multiple religious understandings. I am the spouse of a practicing Muslim, a Buddhist mindfulness and meditation practitioner, an agnostic skeptical of today's face of American Christianity, and a humanist who believes in the potential of our species to bring healing and hope through science and reason.

And I've learned that my ego—the "head" part of me that thinks I'm the most brilliant person alive—can quickly take over if I neglect my spirit. In the mix, there's always been that presence, that guiding energy I encountered early in life, calling me inward and downward to silence, to holy listening, to openness and trust, to intentional community.

In that deeper, more soul-filled place, I remember other identities that I embody as Kristina—woman, Puerto Rican, Italian, daughter, sister—and qualities that I embody on this journey—creative, loyal, joyful. Entwined in this knowing, I can more authentically and gracefully embody my calling, doing the things that my soul loves.

Rev. Dr. Kristina Lizardy-Hajbi is Director of the Office of Professional Formation and Term Assistant Professor of Leadership and Formation at Iliff School of Theology in Denver, Colorado. An Ordained Minister in the United Church of Christ, her previous experience includes denominational leadership, higher education administration, church pastoring, and hospital chaplaincy. Kristina can be contacted at klizardy@iliff.edu

To Be Real: An Invitation to Reflect

By Susan Miller

"Real isn't how you are made," said the Skin Horse. *"It's a thing that happens to you. When a child loves you for a long, long time, not just to play with, but REALLY loves you, then you become Real."*

"Does it hurt?" asked the Rabbit.

"Sometimes," said the SkinHorse, for he was always truthful. *"When you are Real you don't mind being hurt."*

"Does it happen all at once, like being wound up," he asked, *"or bit by bit?"*

"It doesn't happen all at once," said the Skin Horse.

"You become. It takes a long time. That's why it doesn't happen often to people who break easily, or have sharp edges, or who have to be carefully kept. Generally, by the time you are Real, most of your hair has been loved off, and your eyes drop out and you get loose in the joints and very shabby. But these things don't matter at all, because once you are Real you can't be ugly, except to people who don't understand."

-- From *The Velveteen Rabbit* by Margery Williams Bianco

That passage from *The Velveteen Rabbit* came to my mind as I reflected on the CRWHE invitation to write an essay about how being involved with this work has influenced my life. I started thinking about how Parker Palmer describes "soul" as our deepest authenticity. Of course, this brought me to asking questions about how I view myself as an authentic human being, as genuine, as "real."

Questioning led me to flesh out a reflection topic that I put together for my work as a small-group facilitator in the Circles Program at the First Unitarian Universalist Church in Dallas, Texas. The work I do at the church is a continuation of my CRWHE work and it refreshes my soul.

Please know that I was not trained in the Humanities nor was I an English major in College. I had a 36-year career teaching mathematics in the community college. Learning to ask good questions about ultimate concerns took me a while. It is not a child loving me for a long, long time, but my dear colleagues in CRWHE who have loved me for a long, long time that makes me more "real."

I share with you here some quotes and questions I have used in Circles, with the hope that you may get an idea about how comfortable I have become in my skin as a result of working in CRWHE. And I invite you into your own reflection:

> *"We have to dare to be ourselves, however frightening or strange that self may prove to be."* **May Sarton**

- What does being real mean to you?

- What can happen if you trade your authenticity for safety?

- Describe a time in your life when you changed yourself to align with another's version of reality.

- Tell about how being real has hurt you.

- Tell how being real has kept you from being hurt.

In a sermon at our church in 2017, Rev. Aaron White said that he could *feel very lonely in a crowd but not if people were being authentic with each other.*

- Describe a time when you felt this kind of loneliness.

- Describe a time when you comfortable with a group of strangers because you were being authentic.

"Because true belonging only happens when we present our authentic, imperfect selves to the world, our sense of belonging can never be greater than our level of self-acceptance."

— Brené Brown, *Daring Greatly: How the Courage to Be Vulnerable Transforms the Way We Live, Love, Parent, and Lead*

- Tell how this might or might not be true for you.

We usually close our Circles with a quote or poem to invite further reflection, so I invite you to reflect on these words from Fyodor Dostoyevsky's *The Brothers Karamazov*:

"Above all, don't lie to yourself. The man who lies to himself and listens to his own lie comes to a point that he cannot distinguish the truth within him, or around him, and so loses all respect for himself and for others. And having no respect he ceases to love."

Susan Miller is a retired Professor of Mathematics from the Dallas County Community College District and lives in Dallas, Texas, with her husband, Scott. She travels to New England, her childhood home, in the summer to visit family but always returns to her beloved Dallas community of friends and colleagues. She can be reached by email at susanmiller@dcccd.edu

In a Poem

By Jenna Joya Blondel

In a poem, I take up the key
to the garden of my heart
and enter - such sadness -
only bare branches, cold ground.

I walk to a pool of still water,
and look into the depths,
but the water is streaked and dark,
and at the bottom of the pool
lies a bleeding woman.

Do I pull her from the water?
Do I tear my dress to bind her wounds?

Night falls. I stand
and look into the water.

I do not know the ending to this poem.

But the Beloved knows.

And so, in a poem, I sit,
catching the shimmering reflections,
of faces I do not know,
catching them in my hands, like fish,
dripping them on the ground,
pouring them over my head -
a baptism in my own name.

And then, the water is clear and still.
The woman in the pool is gone.

I take off my dress of tears,
and put on a garment of love,
with red roses at my wrists and throat,
and I dance with the One I did not know,
and the garden blooms and sings.

Now, in a poem, dear reader,
take back the key to the garden of your heart.
Wash the blood of sacrifice from the stones.
Let monarch butterflies winter there,
like blossoms in the bare trees.

And spring will make your heart a scented garden
heavy with jasmine, pale in the darkness.
Here is no crown of thorns, only roses for your hair.

Crocuses bloom in your footprints,
and your lips and hands become saffron,
giving golden fragrance to the bread of the world.

You are walking with the Beloved there -
and the Beloved wears your own face.

In your eyes
are water lilies, blooming.
Let yourself see.

Jenna Joya Blondel, Ph.D., Minister of Walking Prayer, has worked as a high school teacher and college professor, in the US and the Middle East, teaching English, ESL, Peace Studies, and Mindfulness Meditation. She loves to travel, especially to Oaxaca, and loves to practice Tai Chi and dance, especially with her husband. She can be contacted by email: jennajoya@gmail.com

The Second Mandala

Being in Community

13 Ways of Looking at Community (...with a 14th thrown in for free)

By Parker J. Palmer

I. Whether we know it or not, like it or not, honor it or not, we are embedded in community. Whether we think of ourselves as biological creatures or spiritual beings or both, the truth remains—we were created in and for a complex ecology of relatedness, and without it we wither and die. This simple fact has a critical implication: community is not a goal to be achieved, but a gift to be received. When we treat community as a product that we must manufacture instead of as a gift we have been given, it will elude us eternally. When we try to "make community happen," driven by desire, design, and determination—places within us where the ego often lurks—we can make a good guess at the outcome: we will exhaust ourselves and alienate each other, snapping the connections we yearn for. Too many relationships have been diminished or destroyed by a drive toward "community-building," which evokes a grasping that is the opposite of what we need to do; relax into our created condition and receive the gift we have been given.

II. Of course, in our culture—a culture premised on the notion that we must manufacture whatever we want or need—learning to relax and receive a gift requires hard work! But the work of becoming receptive is quite unlike the external work of building communal structures, or gathering endlessly to "share" and "solve problems": receptivity involves inner work. Community begins not externally but in the recesses of the human heart. Long before community can be manifest in outward relationship, it must be present in the individual as a "capacity for connectedness"—a capacity to resist the forces of disconnection with which our culture and our psyches are riddled, forces with names like narcissism, egotism, jealousy, competition, empire-building, nationalism, and related forms of madness in which psychopathology and political pathology become powerfully intertwined.

III. We cultivate a capacity for connectedness through contemplation. By this I do not necessarily mean sitting cross-legged and chanting a mantra, though that may work for some. By contemplation I mean any way one has of penetrating the illusion of separateness and touching the reality of interdependence. In my life, the deepest forms of contemplation have been failure, suffering, and loss. When I flourish, it is easy to maintain the illusion of separateness, easy to imagine that I alone am responsible for my good fortune. But when I fall, I see a secret hidden in plain sight: I need other people for comfort, encouragement, and support, and for criticism, challenge, and collaboration. The self-sufficiency I feel in success is a mirage. I need community—and, if I open my heart, I have it.

IV. The most common connotation for the word "community" in our culture is "intimacy," but this is a trap. When community is reduced to intimacy, our world shrinks to a vanishing point: with how many people can one be genuinely intimate in a lifetime? My concept of community must be capacious enough to embrace everything from my relations to strangers I will never meet (e.g., the poor around the world to whom I am accountable), to people with whom I share local resources and must learn to get along (e.g., immediate neighbors), to people I am related to for the purpose of getting a job done (e.g., coworkers and colleagues). Intimacy is neither possible nor necessary across this entire range of relationships. But the capacity for connectedness is both possible and necessary if we are to inhabit the larger, and truer, community of our lives.

V.   The concept of community must embrace even those we perceive as "the enemy." In 1974, I set off on a 14-year journey of living in intentional communities. By 1975, I had come up with my definition of community: "Community is that place where the person you least want to live with always lives." By 1976, I had come up with my corollary to that definition: "And when that person moves away, someone else arises immediately to take his or her place." The reason is simple: relationships in community are so close and so intense that it is easy for us to project onto another person that which we cannot abide in ourselves. As long as I am there, the person I least want to live with will be there as well: in the immortal words of Pogo, "We has met the enemy and it is us." That knowledge is one of the difficult but redeeming gifts community has to offer.

VI. Hard experiences—such as meeting the enemy within, or dealing with the conflict and betrayal that are an inevitable part of living closely with others—are not the death knell of community; they are the gateway into the real thing. But we will never walk through that gate if we cling to a romantic image of community as the Garden of Eden. After the first flush of romance, community is less like a garden and more like a crucible. One stays in the crucible only if one is committed to being refined by fire. If we seek community merely to be happy, the seeking will end at the gate. If we want community to confront the unhappiness we carry within ourselves, the experiment may go on, and happiness—or better, a sense of at-homeness—may be its paradoxical outcome.

VII. It is tempting to think of hierarchy and community as opposites, as one more "either-or." But in mass society, with its inevitable complex organizations, our challenge is to think "both-and," to find ways of inviting the gift of community within those hierarchical structures. I am not proposing the transformation of bureaucracies into communities, which I regard as an impossible dream. I am proposing "pockets of possibility" within bureaucratic structures, places where people can live and work differently than the way dictated by the organization chart. The most creative of our institutions already do this; e.g. those high-tech companies that must organize efficiently to protect the bottom line and get the product out the door, but must also create spaces where people can collaborate in dreaming, playing, thinking wild thoughts, and taking outrageous risks, lest tomorrow's product never be imagined.

VIII. Contrary to popular opinion, community requires leadership, and it requires more leadership, not less, than bureaucracies. A hierarchical organization, with its well-defined roles, rules, and relationships, is better able to operate on automatic pilot than is a community, with its chaotic and unpredictable energy field. But leadership for community is not exercised through the power (i.e., through the use of sanctions) that is the primary tool of bureaucratic leadership. Leadership for community requires authority, a form of power that is freely granted to the leader by his or her followers. Authority is granted to people who are perceived as authentic, as authoring their own words and actions rather than proceeding according to some organizational script. So the authority to lead toward community can emerge from anyone in an organization—and it may be more likely to emerge from people who do not hold positional power.

IX. Leadership for community consists in creating, holding, and guarding a trustworthy space in which human resourcefulness may be evoked. A critical assumption is hidden in that definition—the assumption that people are resourceful. Standard organizational models assume that people have deficits and scarcities rather than resources: people do not want to work, so the organization must surround them with threats; people would not know what to do with the unexpected, so organizational life must be routine; people will try to cheat if given half a chance, so the organization must build walls of security. When we act on the scarcity assumption, it becomes a self-fulfilling prophecy through a process called resentment (small wonder!), and people are rendered incapable of community, at least temporarily, sometimes permanently.

X. Ironically, we often resist leaders who call upon our resourcefulness. We find it threatening when leaders say, "I am not going to tell you how to do this, let alone do it for you, but I am going to create a space in which you can do it for yourselves." Why is that threatening? Because many of us have been persuaded by institutions ranging from educational to industrial to religious that we do not have the resources it takes to do things, or even think things, for ourselves (which, to the extent that we believe it, expands an institution's power over our lives). Many people have been convinced of their own inadequacy, and any leader who wants to invite them into a community of mutual resourcefulness must see this invisible wound and try to heal it.

XI.   Seeing and treating that wound takes courage and tenacity; while the leader is calling followers to fullness, the followers are accusing the leader of not doing his or her job. Every teacher who has tried to create a space for self-sustaining learning community knows this story: students resist on the grounds that "we are not paying tuition to listen to John and Susie talk, but to take notes from you, the person with the Ph.D." It takes a deeply-grounded leader—a leader with a source of identity independent of how popular he or she is with the group—to hold a space in which people can discover their resources while those same people resist, angrily accusing the leader of not earning his or her keep.

XII.   In the face of resistance, an ungrounded leader will revert to the bureaucratic model, the teacher will revert to lecturing rather than inviting inquiry, the manager will revert to rule making rather than inviting creativity. In the face of resistance, leaders will do what they are taught to do—not create space for others, but fill the space themselves—fill it with their own words, their own skills, their own deeds, and their own ego. This, of course, is precisely what followers expect from leaders, and that expectation prolongs the period during which leaders of community must hold the space—hold it in trust until people trust the leader, and themselves, enough to enter it.

XIII. There is a name for what leaders experience during this prolonged period of patient waiting. It is called "suffering" (which is the root meaning for the word "patience"). Suffering is what happens when you see the possibilities in others while they deny those same possibilities in themselves. Suffering is what happens when you hold in trust a space for community to emerge, but others lack the trust to enter the space and receive the gift. Suffering is what happens while you wait out their resistance, believing that people have more resources than they believe they have. But leaders do not want to suffer. So we create and maintain institutional arrangements that protect leaders from suffering by assuming the worst of the followers and encouraging leaders to dominate them by means of power.

XIV. I have yet to see a seminar in suffering as part of a leadership-training program. I can think of three reasons why: (1) we train leaders for bureaucracy rather than community, no matter what we say we are doing; (2) the idea of leadership is still so steeped in machismo that we do not want to acknowledge a "weakness" like suffering; (3) suffering is a spiritual problem, and we want to keep leadership training in the orderly realm of theory and technique, rather than engage in the raw messiness of the human heart.

But leadership for community will always break our hearts. So if we want to lead this way, we must help each other deal with that fact. We might begin by viewing the problem through the lens of paradox, that spiritual way of seeing that turns conventional wisdom upside down. Here, "breaking your heart" (which we normally understand as a destructive process that leaves one's heart in fragments) is reframed as the breaking open of one's heart into larger, more generous forms—a process that goes on and on until the heart is spacious enough to hold a vision of hope and the reality of resistance with tightening like a fist.

If we are willing to embrace the spiritual potential of suffering, then community and leadership, human resourcefulness and the capacity to hold it in trust, will prove to be abundant among us—gifts we have been given from the beginning, but are still learning how to receive.

Parker J. Palmer is a writer, teacher and activist who works independently on issues in education, community, leadership, spirituality, and social change. Founder and Senior Partner of the Center for Courage & Renewal, he has authored 11 books, including *The Courage to Teach, Let Your Life Speak, A Hidden Wholeness, Healing the Heart of Democracy, and most recently, On the Brink of Everything: Grace, Gravity & Getting Old.* He holds a Ph.D. in sociology from the University of California at Berkeley, and his work has been recognized with 13 honorary doctorates and the William Rainey Harper Award, whose previous recipients include Margaret Mead, Elie Wiesel, Paolo Freire.

One Conversation at a Time

By Praveena Dhayanithy

The first day of class every semester is often a juggling act.

That first day is the all-important one for creating the expectations for the days to come, getting to know everyone around me, collecting information, and many other tasks that are "best done first"! I needed to find a balance between delivering the content and hearing from multiple voices. From ideas gathered through conversations with my colleagues and teaching conferences, I created a mandatory one-on-one conversation with my students during the first two weeks of class.

After the "Tell me about yourself" part, I use these conversations to emphasize how to find resources for success. The initial intention is for these conversations to help us get to know each other and to create a safe space for continued dialogue.

In what then felt like a parallel world, my co-worker introduced me to the works of Dr. Parker Palmer. The professional retreats were akin to showers for the brain, helping me reflect inward on important questions about life and work. This process did bring about a period of discomfort as I realized that I needed to slow down while interacting with others. It was a revelation to me that there were questions beyond those that satisfied my curiosity, and these were the questions that best served the interests of the person with whom I was interacting.

It is not uncommon to find among community college students

the single mother struggling to find affordable daycare as she attends classes, the veteran trying to transition to civilian life and the first-generation student who has no one in her family to offer first-hand advice. These are people who have surmounted significant roadblocks just to get to the classroom. They are determined to make a difference in their lives through education. My classroom, I realized, is the best place to seek out ways I can make a difference in the world, while still sustaining my original purpose.

As I carried on these conversations with my students, I began to practice the principles of careful listening and building trusting relationships. For instance, Mia was very silent during the first conversation: I realized she was reflecting inwards in the space of silence. But she did return to talk several times after. Towards the end of the semester, she revealed that she had to endure torture and starvation, fleeing from her country and spending several years in relocation camps, before she could find stability.

In my role as teacher, it took some effort for me to move away from fixing, advising and correcting to turning to wonder and compassionate inquiry. Ted was in despair when he met me in my office as he had not completed several assignments. Instead of giving him the black-and-white consequences this would have on his grade, I asked him what his reaction to the situation taught him. After assuring him that he did hear me right, he reflected on this for a while and told me that he cared enough to bounce back from the current grade he had. He went on to create a solid action plan to stay on top of upcoming deadlines.

My experiences with the work of CRWHE retreats and the writing of Parker Palmer have enabled me to help Mia and Ted build deep connections and resilience in the face of challenges. In a world that feels divided, the need to feel empowered as a community increases substantially. Caring about teaching and about students brings joy to the day. In order to stay true to our professions and our inner truth, it is important to create and sustain safe spaces for courageous conversations, one conversation at a time.

Praveena Dhayanithy is Professor of Mathematics at Richland College in Dallas, TX. She enjoys her work in the area of Mathematics and empowering students to succeed. Praveena is actively involved with group facilitation, planning and designing retreats for reflection and renewal. She can be reached at PDhayanithy@dcccd.edu

My Messy Garden
By Pamala Gist

As a child, I spent my summer vacations with my "Granny." She was my mentor, storyteller, and best friend. Granny grew up in the country where she left school after the sixth grade and began working in the fields to help her family. Although she moved to town when she married my grandfather, her farming roots never left her.

Each spring, Granny planted a large vegetable garden in the big lot behind her house. As her constant shadow in the summers, I learned that growing a garden was a long hard process. I watched her break the black soil with a rusty hand plow and make neat rows, lined up perfectly. I can still see the back of her old-fashioned bonnet as she stooped over, placing seeds tenderly and lovingly into the rich soil as if blessing each one. She carefully hand-watered everything, carrying her bucket and dipper from plant to plant. Sometimes she sang softly while working, most often the old gospel, "Bread of Heaven/Feed me 'til I want no more."

I lingered near her daily because I knew she would tell me stories, often about her childhood on the farm or her many cats, all with distinct personalities. She gave new meaning to familiar tales and Bible stories as she added her own colorful images and dialogue. I would listen while she worked, not realizing that her stories were planting a different kind of garden.

By summer, she had row upon row of peas, carrots, beans, squash, and even watermelon fattening in the blistering Texas sun. Each row seemed to grow perfectly synchronized in its own time: onions first, then tomatoes, and finally, okra and black eyes maturing late in the hottest part of summer. No weeds dared poke their heads up in my grandmother's garden, because she was up at dawn, attacking new sprouts with her sharp hoe.

Every evening I wandered along behind Granny as we picked the ripe squash and peas that were destined for tomorrow's dinner or canning. She fed her whole family the entire year with those vegetables grown with love. Summers with her gave me my sense of what a perfect garden should look like.

Unfortunately, my Granny's green thumb did not pass down to me. Oh, I love the idea of gardening, but my rows look like crooked back-country roads. Bugs feast on my plants, reducing them to sticks. My flowers turn yellow, wilt, and die from neglect or overwatering. Weeds crowd out useful plants. I have planted many a spring garden that someone else had to take over so I wouldn't lose everything.

STARBURST THINKING

It was years before I understood that my inability to focus on something as simple as a garden came from a condition called "attention deficit disorder," one I laughingly labeled "starburst thinking." My scattered mind impacted my daily work life as a Division Dean at Cedar Valley College, resulting in what seemed to me to be a chaotic mess. I somehow managed to teach, develop faculty, attend meetings, write proposals, and run a division, even though I consistently lost things, went off on random side trips when teaching, spent too much time chatting with faculty, arrived late to meetings, and was unable to stay focused on anything.

In an effort to "cure" my attention deficit disorder in my role as teacher and administrator, I color-coded my files, only to forget which color represented what subject. I routinely sketched during long meetings to keep my mind from running off into deep space. I wrote out my lectures word for word and tried hard to stick to my script. More often than not, a student's comment or a current event would pull the entire class into a rowdy dialogue only vaguely related to the lesson for the day. Every day was a battle between the structured needs of an organized institution and my disordered mind.

A FORMATION RETREAT

Sometime later, I attended a spring formation retreat offered by the Center for Formation in the Community College that centered around the theme of gardens. We were invited to read poems about gardens and plant seeds; we looked at pictures of puffy hyacinths, colorful roses, and cute petunias, none yellowed or withered. As a grand finale, we were given the afternoon to create the garden of our life, in art or poetry. I immediately resented this activity, because I knew that my life did not look like any kind of garden.

As I pondered the exercise, my frustration grew. I tried to imagine my own metaphorical garden, but my mind could only pull up weeds, dead leaves, bugs, and spent flowers. I remembered my Granny's and compared it to my own. As the minutes ticked by that afternoon, I stared at photographs of gardens, then glanced at fellow retreat participants happily focused on making collages, drawing flowers, or creating other crafty masterpieces. I was the only one still thumbing through photos. At one point I almost gave up on finding something to represent my life.

Then I turned over a picture and my search stopped. A large stand of aspen trees, randomly growing on the side of a mountain, flamed gold in the afternoon sunlight. The forest had no balance or order, no straight lines or perfect angles. The white trunks were crooked and pockmarked with black scars. But there they stood, beautiful and perfect as if planted by a cosmic gardener with a sacred-but-mysterious plan, one that no one else could see.

I immediately knew that cluster of aspens represented my garden. I quickly took out watercolors, painted several white trunks against a blue sky and added branches with black marks on them. Then I covered the branches with vivid golden and yellow splotches and scattered a few spots on the ground, near the roots. There was no symmetry, rigidity, or perspective in my painting; it emerged naturally, one tree at a time, each one creating its own beauty among the others.

For the first time, I could see the garden that was my life.

GROWING IN ITS OWN TIME

When invited to show our work, my painting was different from any of the others, eliciting some confused looks. That exercise changed my perspective about work and life. I no longer scolded myself for not being like other division deans and began nurturing my own roots. I stopped hiding my unorthodox ideas in fear they would be misunderstood and began incorporating them into proposals and strategic planning. Some of those messy ideas brought millions of dollars to our college. I stopped criticizing myself for spending so much time wandering halls, talking with faculty and students, and let myself enjoy those priceless walks. My heart knew that my garden would grow in its own time, just as those golden aspens shining in the sun.

I learned to appreciate all manner of successful teaching, as I watched faculty members create, improvise, use unusual methods, or venture away from their syllabi. If their methods worked with students, then the outcome spoke for itself. With students, I recognized that often creative ones left the most mistakes on their papers: a misplaced comma, misspelled words, or sentence fragments. I began to look for the garden they were growing in their writing and told them, "Just write. We'll fix the mistakes later."

Amazingly, the method worked. I also stopped forcing students to turn in formal outlines before they started writing and expanded research topics to allow them to nurture their own interests. I asked the kind of open-ended questions I'd learned in retreat, ones that pushed them to grow their own ideas and tell their own stories, rather than my telling them the stories I knew.

I realized that everyone has a unique garden. Very few look like my Granny's, but each has its own beauty. Now retired, I look back on the garden that I planted at my college after that spring retreat. It was messy at first. Many colleagues couldn't fathom the seedlings I was setting out, just as my painting of that golden mountainside confused retreatants. However, our division developed the reputation of the "most peaceful division on campus." When I made my daily visit to the fine arts building, students stopped me to talk about their next recital or latest art work showing in the gallery. My own students wrote tearful thank-you notes on their final exams, using words like "encouraged" and "inspired." Many told me that they'd always hated English until they were in my class.

When I announced my retirement, faculty members thanked me for listening to them and for recognizing the beauty in their own teaching methods rather than trying to force them into a preset idea of what time in a classroom should look like. As I walked through the campus one last time, I passed labs and classrooms with shiny new equipment funded by grants that I had developed. I smiled inwardly at my name on the placard outside the new art gallery, a place dedicated to student work, a dream come true for the department.

The insight I garnered at that formation retreat enabled me to claim my unique gardening gifts. Today the garden I started is larger than I could have imagined, filled with numerous golden trees standing proud on their mountainside.

My Granny, if she were here to see it, would be proud.

Pamela Gist held many titles during her 30 years at Cedar Valley College in Dallas: English Faculty, Director of Special Populations, Dean of Resource Development, and Executive Dean of Liberal and Fine Arts. Yet she still says that she is first and foremost "just a teacher." Now retired and living in Arizona, she enjoys traveling, writing stories, and spending time with her four grandchildren, her partner of 40 years, and her two dogs. She can be reached at pgist@dcccd.edu

Courage Memories
By Susan Barkley

Memories of formation work are one of its greatest gifts, constant companions on the journey towards wholeness.

A strong memory of what has touched me most in the Courage to Teach Formation Retreats is that of a movement toward honoring self and others.

I remember one specific activity where we were asked to bring a childhood picture that we loved. Who was that little boy or girl? What endeared them to a favorite aunt or best friend? What birthright gifts were evident right from the beginning? To envision our birthright gifts—those gifts that are our innate wealth and beauty—has helped me to rediscover my uniqueness and to embrace myself.

The Buddhists have a term, *maitri,* which means loving-kindness toward ourselves; trusting the basic goodness of who we are and our inner wisdom. What I have discovered is that when we become more at peace with ourselves, it is easy to honor others. We become more patient, less controlling, and more open to all of life. We begin to look with wonder.

So our journey has been to rediscover who we were from the beginning. T.S. Eliot writes of this:

> **We shall not cease from exploration**
> **And the end of all our exploring**
> **Will be to arrive where we started**
> **And know the place for the first time.**

Another memory of the years in formation work that I will always carry with me is the abundance I have felt in community. Focusing on abundance and not scarcity helps us to become aware that we do not have to have all of the gifts or do all of the work. We can rely on others to support and supplement our gifts. The only thing we must **not** do is to hold back the unique gifts we have to offer. I love the way Robert Frost names this in *The Gift Outright*:

> **Something we were withholding made us weak**
> **Until we found out that it was ourselves**
> **We were withholding from our land of living,**
> **And forthwith found salvation in surrender.**

Wholeness is a journey, not a destination. Thanks to formation work, I am on solid footing on the journey.

Susan Barkley is Executive Dean of the School of World Languages, Cultures and Communications. In addition to her administrative position she has also taught French, ESOL, and Travel and Tourism as well as facilitating many faculty professional development sessions. Global Education is one of her areas of responsibility and highest priority. Having once been a travel consultant her greatest delight is traveling around the world. She resides in Dallas, Texas. She can be reached at Sbarkley@dcccd.edu

A Thin Place

By Deb Yoder

Perfect peace.

Those words gently resonate within me as I pull the covers up to my chin and roll over to snuggle into the warm spot in my bed.

Perfect peace. I hear it again.

Gently whispered but clearly important. The words come from within me, from a thin place inside myself. I don't "think" of it; instead, the words are just there as a precious gift.

It is 6:30 in the morning. The house is quiet. Sitting now in my favorite chair sipping the first cup of coffee of the morning, I can barely hear a train in the distance. I remember a scripture I read many years ago: "You keep me in perfect peace when my mind is stayed on You."

How would life be if more moments were bathed in perfect peace?

Peace I leave with you not as the world gives but as I give. Those words gently float across my mind leaving its caress lingering sweetly in the air I breathe. Nourishment for my thirsty soul is in each breath.

For a moment my thoughts attempt to distract me, pulling me to the things I need to "do" today. I resist. To be in this moment, this place of perfect peace is far more delightful than any other thought. It is a calm delight, truly a thin place where heaven and earth feel very close.

Every morning, for as long as I can remember, my first waking thoughts contained a sense of urgency.

Get up! You have lots to do. You are behind in preparing for your upcoming classes. You still haven't written that report that should have been done weeks ago. And, oh yeah, how in the world are you going to pay all these bills…how…with all the debt you are already under? Are you sure about what you're doing anyway? Get up! Get busy! You have to figure all this stuff out!

It occurs to me now as the steam tickles my nose as I sip on my second cup of coffee… just breathe. The answers are not in "Get up! Get busy! Do something!"

The answers are in the stillness. In this quiet, effortless being. Being fully present in this moment now.

SLOW MORNINGS CREATE THE SPACE

As a teacher of mindfulness, it has become my practice to start my mornings slowly, to set my intention to be aware, present, and peaceful throughout the day. No matter how many years I have been engaged in formation work, no matter how many heartfelt attempts to live undivided, I find that I'm still frequently tested. This morning gifts me with one of those pop quizzes the Universe sends to keep me humble.

As I listen to calming music on the hour drive to campus, I feel well prepared for my 9:30 psychology class. Today's topic is consciousness, one of my favorites, because it gives me the opportunity to share practical insights that may help my students experience life with less anxiety, a dose of self-compassion, and empathy for others.

My outline is ready along with an interactive PowerPoint with relevant video clips. The bumper-to-bumper traffic doesn't upset me. I happily let other drivers merge into my lane. Once parked, I stroll to my office, appreciative the Texas heat has subsided and the trees are wearing their stunning fall colors.

Poised and still quite peaceful, I walk mindfully to the classroom where 100 eager young minds wait.

Then, here comes the test of my intention. The computer does not work. The projector does not work. The audio does not work. I remain calm trying the fixes that usually work, but, to no avail, and finally call the tech support office.

I get the answering machine.

Still fairly peaceful, I put the students in learning groups and offer some initial questions for them to discuss. Then I head to the tech support office. That's when the inner dialogue begins! *Come on already! This is like the fifth time this semester that nothing works.* I take a few more strides. *How come nobody answered the phone? If they had answered, I could have stayed with my class.*

I knock loudly on the office door. When no one responds, I go in and hunt for someone. I find a young man who appears annoyed that I interrupted him enjoying his breakfast taco. I try my best to be polite as I ask for help. He follows me to the classroom, tinkers with the computer, and within minutes blurts out, "It ain't happenin' today."

I hear myself reply, "Thank you for trying. Perhaps you can fix it before my next class on Thursday." In my head another script runs, *Come on, buddy! This is your job!*

CHANGE OF PLANS

As the techie leaves the room, I return to my lesson on awareness. I know my body language and my unintentional scowl betray my "acceptance" of a change of plans. I stop mid-sentence, look at my students in the eyes:

"Let's really practice awareness. What am I feeling right now?"

Without hesitation, a normally reserved student says, "Frustrated!"

Another adds, "Disappointed."

A third more forthright voice offers, "You're pissed!"

"Okay. So now that you are aware and I am aware of this negative emotion, what's the grown-up thing to do here?"

The test that confronted me that day turns into the lesson. I ask my students to problem-solve this situation. A shy baseball player says, "Just send us the links to the videos." The class applauds his great idea.

Others chime in, "Just breathe, Dr. Yoder. We like your stories better anyway."

We laugh. I say out loud, "I'm not mad anymore."

They know already. We laugh again.

SEEING THE STORY WE ARE IN

That day, my students learn that unrecognized and uncontrolled emotion can lead us to hurt others or engage in irrational behavior. Rather than employing our more rational minds to solve problems, we behave like undisciplined toddlers, throw fits, sulk, or demand revenge.

Unfortunately, to the detriment of ourselves and others, we often rehearse a perceived injustice over and over until a slight becomes a storm in our minds. Simply becoming aware of our emotional state and naming it out loud has the phenomenal effect of diminishing its control over us.

Parker Palmer teaches that the journey toward an undivided life, a life of wholeness, requires facing our shadow and light. The challenge in the classroom that day caused me to think, feel, and do things contrary to who I am and how I want to show up in the world. Perhaps it is my shadow showing up as ego, that darker self-centered, self-important imposter that prevents me from being present, empathic, and peaceful.

When recounting the morning's events, a colleague reminded me that we all have a story. The tech office had recently lost a long-time team member to cancer. The guy who came to my class was dealing with health issues in addition to being overwhelmed by the loss of his friend.

What followed was shame. Damn. How do I now get loose from shame?

I recognize it just as I do other emotions. Name it, resolve to choose compassion, consider the others' perspective, and let it go. Such a process requires forgiving myself and if I have harmed another, asking for her or his forgiveness.

It also requires self-compassion. I remember Thomas Moore's words from *Care of the Soul*:

"If we can see the story we are in when we fall into our various compulsive behaviors and moods, then we might know how to move through them more freely and with less distress."

As I slow down and breathe, I am reminded that in the midst of life's small frustrations and major challenges, I can pause and become aware of that thin place inside myself. A place of calmness, wholeness, and peace. A place from which I can make better choices and take creative action. Where heaven and earth come very close. Time has a way of losing its urgency. There is peace.

Such places show up even in the classroom, gracing me with life's energy, empowering me to listen deeply, love well, and enabling me to be who I want to be. Often, I stumble upon thin places as they unexpectedly, gently rescue me from the hustle, reminding me to just breathe and experience being loved, connected, free, unencumbered—like being wrapped in a warm blanket in front of a cozy fire with nowhere else to be, nothing else to do.

Dr. Debra M. Yoder, psychology professor at Mountain View College and the University of North Texas at Dallas, has a counseling and consulting practice, is a Certified Daring Way™ Facilitator and Formation Facilitator. Deb lives in Rockwall, Texas, where she enjoys playing golf with her husband, Byron Gillory and their sons and daughter. She can be contacted through email: drdebyoder@gmail.com at Harvest Works, LLC or dyoder@dcccd.edu

Weaving

By Jackie Claunch

There is a thread you follow.

William Stafford, *The Way It Is*

My daughter, Gina, was, as a young woman,
A weaver,
Spinning from raw wool,
Coloring from hues of earth and flowers,
The threads, weaving them together
on her loom,
Creating a rich tapestry.

Maybe life is like that,
Some raw material, colored by knowledge
To create a weaving, or perhaps,
A basket full of weavings.

My friends, colleagues, family members,
Here or elsewhere,
Inhabit the weavings of
My story.

But how do I weave together a story? Stafford tells me there is
a thread I follow.

It goes among things that change. But it doesn't change.

It's Fiesta in San Antonio, the Arts Fair,
I stand facing it, a weaving
with hues of sunset – and circles –
Symbolic of the circles that served as
guideposts on a personal and
professional journey,

Blending two selves to come closer to one,
Informing, enhancing the leader within,
Making connections, taking risks.

Building and living in a college culture
Where together we could create and share
Values, mission, vision, learning,
formation and renewal.

I am seeing the circles that marked my own personal journey of
formation and renewal as I follow the thread. My first formal
encounters with circles of trust came in the form of several
overnight retreats at Richland College in the late 1980's, the
brainchild of my good friend, Elaine Sullivan. The goal was
our own development as faculty and other leaders wanting to
meet the learning and support needs of an ever-increasing adult
student population.

Memories of the circle, the candle, the coming
together, of wisdom shared by great teachers,
guiding us to learn by doing, communing with
nature, writing, sharing, listening.

There were for me at first, amidst so many good
writers, feelings of inadequacy, a reluctance to
share what seemed Not good enough.
And so for more than one retreat,

I sat, listening and learning in silence.
But then there came great teachers
like Rica and James,
with experiences to spark creation,
to become a part of my formation,
to guide me on my path.

Did you ever draw a picture with your other
hand, the non-dominant hand, for most the left,
for me the right, we did that day with Rica.
I who could not draw, found myself untethered,
for after all what mattered? What did one expect?
My sketch was not too bad, worth sharing,
reminding me of my finger painting
my fourth grade teacher loved.

From James, learned more of writing in an hour
than all that came before. I remember little of
that brief sojourn, but this – going out, inspired
to breathe into my writing what I saw and felt
around me and coming back to share. As years
passed on a thought of him would prompt a
momentary celebration of what a gift he brought
that day.

In the late 1980's, I discovered *PeerSpirit* with founders,
Christina Baldwin and Ann Linea. Over the next 15 years a
series of experiences with them continued to enhance my own
formation as a leader and facilitator.

**Asheville, North Carolina, then Whidbey Island,
Washington,**

Later, the Island of Hawaii, and with my
husband on Cortez Island.
Personal and professional sojourns
Becoming part of the weaving.

The Circle themes – Nature, retreats,
the center, the candle, the talking pieces, the
tingshaw,
Time for walks in the forest, reflection, writing,
Questions to ponder alone, in dyads, in triads, in
community.

The circle entered my work, not consciously, but, looking back,
I see the connections in the coming together of individuals
to form a shared vision for a Multicultural Center that would
transform the face – the faces – of Richland College. I began
to understand the power of empowering a community and
its individuals to create together, to speak peacefully of our
differences to share a common vision.

Stafford's words continue to speak to me:

There is a thread you follow...

People wonder about what things you are pursuing.

After 23 years of learning from my teachers and mentors, I left
Richland College to embark on a new adventure. Here was the
opportunity to create with others Northwest Vista College, the
fourth of the Alamo Colleges. I recognized through all I had
learned in my circles of teachers and friends that a culture can
create itself but may not be the one desired.

I knew from observation that I had to lead and empower in
order to create the desired culture. Much time together was
given to creating mission, shared vision and values, always

with student success in the forefront. As the years went by, there were also challenges and new opportunities. I remember a particular challenge: my small group of extremely talented leaders that needed to work more effectively together. We tried a retreat – maybe not a great result – except for the tingshaw gift (traditional Tibetan bells).

> **The tingshaw, if well tuned, creates**
> **The resonating sound one may use**
> **To open – and close – a gathering –**
> **The musical echo is a reminder to take a moment**
> **To breathe and to become fully present.**

With the tingshaw, we began a new ritual, perhaps a gift to ourselves. We gathered each week, called into circle by the tingshaw, the host for the week bringing a poem, a quote, the nature cards, an object, what I later came to know as a third thing. We would each then share an insight or feeling and listen to one another, without judgment. Closing with the tingshaw, we'd then adjourn to the meeting room, as human beings with different ways of knowing and being. This gathering practice continued, sometimes with the inclusion of guests, for several years until my retirement. Through time and changing faces, that 20-minute weekly gathering changed the tenor of our meetings – the ways we worked together.

Meanwhile, under the leadership of Sue Jones and Elaine Sullivan, the Center for Renewal and Wholeness (CRWHE) was created and housed at Richland College. I had followed their work and learned about the formation concepts and practices initiated by Parker Palmer.

At some point, I knew it was time to bring the teacher formation and renewal work to Northwest Vista College. I invited two faculty members to attend a facilitator training; then we brought

Elaine Sullivan to work with the new faculty facilitators in the first Formation retreat. The work was joyfully received and began the training of others facilitators and the expansion of the formation and renewal journey at the College. Although I have been retired since 2016, the work at Northwest Vista continues. And so does mine. Stafford continues to remind me:

There is a thread you follow...

You have to explain about the thread.
But it is hard for others to see.

Formation and renewal serve as the circles in my weaving, guiding a culture in which individual members work in community while taking their own journeys of:

> **Learning to be,**
> **Learning to work,**
> **Learning to lead,**
> **Learning to serve...Together.**

As for my personal journey of becoming, I find it in the continuing weaving, threaded in and around the circles of formation. For me, each encounter with Formation and Renewal is a new opportunity.

> **I am in community, connecting with others,**
> **slowing down, exploring deeply**
> **the inner dimensions of my life and work.**
> **I have found my gifts, my shadows,**
> **the writer and artist that lies within,**
> **dared to share from the heart,**
> **where sadness and joy walk hand in hand.**

And so:

>Departed loved ones,
>Mother, Father, Husband, Daughter,
>You are there.
>You are the rose, the hummingbird,
>The butterfly, the wild horse,
>The music, the dance.
>
>Over 70 years – three generations –
>Learning, family, community, being
>Becoming the story.
>
>I see great teachers, wise counselors,
>A passion for learning and service,
>Leaders of past, present and future.
>
>I see fatherhood, motherhood,
>Sisterhood, brotherhood
>And soul mates.
>
>We have celebrated together
>And grieved together.
>We have worked and played together,
>Laughed and cried together,
>Walked, loved nature,
>Left divots on the golf course,
>Found music that touched the soul –
>Or made us want to dance.
>We have sat together, lived together,
>Created together.

We have learned I think,
Great leadership, from wherever it comes,
Is not about power.
But about *empowerment.*

Weaving the threads now, creating meaning out of this cloth of a lifetime, holding in my heart all those who inhabit the weavings of my story, I continue to be grateful for Stafford's constant reminder in my life to never let go of the thread:

Nothing you do can stop times unfolding.
But you don't ever let go of the thread.

Dr. Jackie Claunch spent 40 years in community college education, first at Richland College, then as founding President of the Alamo Colleges Northwest Vista College. She considers herself blessed to have been able to discover and follow her passion for serving community college students in pursuit of their life dreams. Nowadays one might find her hiking, gardening, golfing, traveling, hanging out with friends or family, or even facilitating a retreat. She can be reached at jclaunch3535@icloud.com

First Breath, Last Breath

By Theresa Garfield

Breathe.

Facing a never-ending barrage of interruptions delivered through a device the size of the palm of my hand, laden with electromagnetic impulses, images, sounds, and 24-7 access to the world in which we live, I find it challenging to be still, to reflect, and to

Breathe.

The first breath of my day brings with it hope, promise, and the ability to conquer anything. The second, a little less certain, but still hopeful. By mid-day my breath becomes intentional, driven, labored. By nightfall, it becomes a quiet gasp. By bedtime, a long sigh.

Breathe.

The first breath of a newborn is a celebration, filled with anticipation and promise. The fast-paced breath of two lovers is passionate. The absence of breath while waiting for final word, bated. The last breath of a relative or celebrated friend is empty, reflective, final.

Breathe.

Dr. Theresa Garfield, an Associate Professor at Texas A&M University-San Antonio, is a proud mother of her daughter, Audrey, and "dog" mom to Millie and Shotzie. She enjoys debating, learning, and mentoring others. She can be reached at theresagarfield13@gmail.com

Transformations in an Inner-City School

By Mindy Manes

Classes had just ended for the summer at our inner-city high school in Kansas City, Kansas—a city whose murder rate now exceeds that of Chicago. The campus sits in the heart of gang territory. I'd completed my first year as the school's Restorative Justice Facilitator and was cleaning up my room when I came across a tattered red spiral notebook. There was no name on it. One of the students, however, had neatly printed these words:

> *For you to trust in your heart of hearts you must be willing to walk down the loneliest road because very few people are willing to indure the PAIN the SCARAFACE and DILIGENCE to be successful because it's a up hill battle and along that road your not going to see too many friends your going to see your shadow most often.*

> *For you to fight your way through this fight is by putting in effort because effort gets you noticed, effort gets your mother out the ghetto, effort provides for your mother in child and effort will get you seen on tape. Which is a battle between you, in yourself. Nobody else can't give you effort Because at the end of the day we not taking a 100 shots we making a 100 shots   that's mind set . . . That's mind set.*

Let me provide a context for this pupil's work. Our alternative school receives 75 students each year, kids who've been removed from the Kansas City high schools because they're failing and falling too far behind to graduate. Many of them have been repeatedly suspended for fighting and truancy. Jail time is often a common denominator. They're either directly involved with gangs or tangentially affected by them.

The students coming to us have been scarred by trauma. They live in an American war zone, 20 minutes away from the affluent suburbs where I safely reside with scarcely a care. Before starting this job, I would daily watch stories about Kansas City murders on the local news, feeling my heart touched; however, they would remain "over there" in my mind. Now I pay close attention to each story knowing that when I go to school the next day, I will learn *how*—not *if*—but *how* that victim was related to our students…neighbor, friend, former classmate or family member.

The stresses these kids experience are unbelievable. A student who, while talking on the phone with his father, hears him being stabbed. A girl whose little sister is shot in the head by another young child on the playground. A student whose nephew is killed in the backseat of his car during a random drive-by shooting. A sleeping mother is shot through her wall when a gang retaliation targets the wrong house. A gentle, sweetheart of a boy who falls apart at school because he has opened his door to gang members who have come for his two brothers: the gang members execute the brothers in a nearby park.

These are just some of the stories I heard during my first couple of months working at the school. And yet, despite their traumas, these kids showed up and worked with grit and determination to earn their degrees. In my first year at this school, I watched students go through life-changing transformations, from hopelessness to graduating with solid plans for their future careers.

During the 2017-18 school year, this "high truancy" population had an 81-90% attendance rate because students wanted to come to a place filled with people they viewed as "family." Despite the innate volatility of this population, there was not a single fight at the school during this same time frame, and only 13 students had to be suspended for a while to cool off. Since 2016, the graduation rate tripled, with a waiting list of students who now want to attend.

One of the reasons our students succeed, I believe, rests with the dedication of our principal and his team who strive to create strong, respectful relationships. The first day of school, most students enter the building with their defenses up, careful not to make eye contact, deliberately rebuffing connections with others. But by the end of the first week, most open up dramatically, buoyed by the respect and genuine caring with which the staff treats them.

RESTORATIVE JUSTICE

Restorative justice empowers students to resolve conflicts by personally addressing their actions and the consequences their actions have on others, then making amends. Its roots originate with indigenous peoples from Maori and North America. A growing practice at schools and in courtrooms throughout the United States and other countries, it has been found effective at creating genuine accountability and lasting change in people's behaviors.

Before going to work as a Restorative Justice Facilitator, I'd never had any training or experience in a teaching capacity. For years I'd been the Chief Operating Officer (COO) for the Edison Awards, a marketing organization known as the "Oscars of Innovation." During that time, I'd also mediated cases in court on a volunteer basis. After the 2016 election that revealed such deep divides in our country, I recognized a personal need to build bridges on more than just a volunteer basis. When the Heartland Mediators Association sent out a notice for a Restorative Justice Facilitator position at an inner-city school, I was intrigued. After visiting the school and meeting its students and dedicated team, I knew it was the place I wanted to be. The principal felt that my mediation experience, circle of trust work, and years as a mom and Girl Scout leader had prepared me for this role. I made the leap from the business world to education. And when I left school at the end of each day, my heart felt light with the rightness of that choice.

LIFE IN A MASH UNIT

Before my COO role, I'd worked at Johnson County Community College (JCCC) as an Innovation Strategist where I'd been trained in Parker Palmer's circle of trust retreat model by the Center for Renewal and Higher Education. During that same time, I was also trained as a Kansas Supreme Court-approved mediator. I found much overlap between mediation and Palmer's work, particularly the holding of space for people to find their own answers.

At JCCC, I'd helped colleagues facilitate staff development retreats that taught reflective practices and invited inner personal work. We spent months developing themes and activities, crafting perfect questions and finding just the right quotes and poems to create an optimal experience—a luxury that my perfectionist soul loved.

Soon after I arrived at the alternative high school, I realized that the training I'd gotten when I was at JCCC was somewhat like preparing a person to be a precise, perfect brain surgeon…and then throwing her into a MASH unit. A couple of hours into my first day, the principal came into my office to tell me that three girls had had an altercation, and he wanted me to create a space for them to resolve the issue. Eager to jump into my new role and thinking about the time I'd need to craft a meaningful experience, I asked, "When do you want that done. Maybe next Thursday?"

"No!" he replied. "In 10 minutes!"

That was how that first year flew by. I had to let go of my need for control and perfection and do "good enough" jobs as they arose.

I saw students one-on-one when teachers sent them to my office. Often they arrived angry about some altercation with a faculty member or fellow student. They fully expected the principal to suspend them or me to enact some kind of punishment or tedious behavior modification. They were completely caught off guard when I asked them to share something they were interested in and then asked if they'd like to watch a video about that subject. Every time I used this technique—literally 100% of the time—a student went from angrily pacing and cursing to a place of peace.

TELL IT SLANT

That is the power, as Palmer writes in *A Hidden Wholeness*, of using Emily Dickinson's "tell it slant" advice rather than hitting a problem head-on. Although it often took some digging, I could usually find resources with a strong motivational message that would fit a student's needs. In addition to helping individual students, our administration is deeply committed to creating community and generating an atmosphere at the school which prevents problems from erupting. Part of my job is facilitating weekly circles which invited personal inner work. Students take turns being my helper and choosing a theme, ensuring we are hearing what the students wanted to address, and that all students' voices are heard.

Although not completely sure which student had written in the notebook I found, I did know that he came from "Group 5," 10 male students who had been creating most of the turmoil in the school. Their classroom was characterized by non-stop loud conversations, arguments, and paper-throwing bedlam. The lead teacher for this group was an ex-Marine who grew up as a tough Detroit street kid and had a huge heart for students.

My role was to facilitate an experience for this group every day, one that prompted self-reflection. The exercises I designed included movies such as *Gridiron Gang*, a film based on the true story of the football team created at the Kilpatrick Detention Center in Los Angeles, followed by a circle during which students were asked to ponder reflective questions.

The boys liked the movies, but they mightily resisted those circles. Within a couple of weeks, however, they learned to listen to each other and themselves. Their self-defeating behaviors began to melt away. They discussed deeply polarizing issues in a manner that could set a much-needed example in our society. For example, the boys had engaged in heated discussions in the classroom over NFL players taking a knee during the anthem. Using the circle process, they respectfully listened to one another, and even when they stepped back from those circle guidelines, the group continued to engage in a reflective, civil dialogue.

Because of their early resistance to our circles, I'd made the mistake of shortening the process by not setting out the symbols that we used in the other classes' circles. Those symbols included a centerpiece and talking stick that the student body had created with words that represented what the school means to them and a vase they'd broken and glued back together. Having the vase on the table reminded students that they, too, could put their lives back together and the cracks would allow their light to shine through. One day, a student in Group 5 told me they needed those symbols, too. After that, I made sure to set them out each time.

As school leadership predicted, when Group 5 students were removed from the other classrooms, student productivity for the rest of the students shot up. What amazed school officials, however, was that Group 5's productivity also increased, gradually doubling, then tripling. These students, assessed in January as extremely unlikely to graduate, walked across the stage on May 23 in front of a standing-room-only crowd of screaming-with-pride family members, many of whom had never finished high school themselves.

I credit their turn-around to several things: their own perseverance in doing deep inner work, the dedication of their lead teacher and the principal, and the motivational videos they saw and then reflected upon. The You-Tube post featuring Los Angeles Lakers basketball star Kobe Bryant which focused on the importance of a work ethic was especially popular. That's the one the student who wrote the passage at the beginning of this story had viewed. The young man had soaked in Kobe's message so deeply that a number of direct quotes found their way onto his pages despite his only having heard them once. So did the reflective questions I'd offered. He'd carefully taped them into the tattered red notebook next to where he'd recorded his thoughts:

> **QUOTE:** *You have to trust in your heart of hearts. Inside—that what you're doing, what you believe in— is a worthy cause, a winnable fight.*

> **QUESTION:** What worthy cause fills your heart of hearts?

> **QUOTE:** *You fight your way through this one, but you do NOT quit. You do not give up on your merit. Do not quit school. Do not quit on your goal, your dreams.*

And we're not just talking about not quitting. We're talking about taking the prize home.

QUESTION: Describe the day you take the prize home.

After one of America's tragic school shootings, my mom and dad asked if I felt safe at my school. I told them that while anything could happen anywhere, I felt far safer at this school than I did in our daughters' huge, affluent, suburban one. At large schools, it's easy for a young person to fall through the cracks. With our smaller number of students and strong focus and attention on each one, we notice when a kid becomes uncharacteristically subdued, is ostracized by other students, or seems angry or hurt—and we reach out.

As a Restorative Justice Facilitator, I end each day feeling at peace in my heart because I've helped create oases of harmony in an overheated world. At our inner-city school, this inner work done by students in their circles is truly transforming lives.

Mindy Manes serves as the Restorative Justice Facilitator for an inner-city school in Kansas City, Kansas. In her free time, she mediates cases at court as a Kansas Supreme Court-approved mediator. She can be contacted by e-mail at manes. mindy@gmail.com

Gifts Wrapped in Grief

by John Millemon

Waking in a hospital bed, I slowly gathered my senses. Two women who I later learned were nurses hovered over me. Looking at a medical chart, one asked, "Who is this man?"

The other replied, "He's the one whose wife and sister died in a car wreck."

Never had I felt so helpless and frightened. My wife, Celia, and my sister, Mary Jane, were the two people I felt closest to. Celia was my first love and best friend. Mary Jane, older and wiser than I, had always been around to offer advice and encouragement.

I'd been a shy man all my life, and now I was all alone.

Growing up I didn't realize how special my surroundings were. Our home and nearby farm contained all the things boys love: bicycles, trail bikes, a motor scooter and a motorcycle. There I could hike, swim, build bridges and dams, play with my dog, horseback ride, and see deer, coyotes, and wild turkeys daily. In addition, our family spent each summer at Lake of the Woods in northern Minnesota, a part of the boundary waters with Canada.

In school, I was an average student. I'd enjoyed playing pick-up sports with childhood friends, but playing on a team in front of crowds frightened me. Instead, I joined the Boy Scouts. The leadership training that organization offered enabled me to become a senior patrol leader and earn Eagle rank.

In many ways my life was idyllic, surrounded by my sister,

parents, aunts, uncles, and cousins who took me under their wings. For example, one uncle gave me flying lessons. Another, who owned a television store, always provided me with the latest in electronics. My sister was always there to encourage and help me explore and evaluate options to solve whatever problem that I was facing.

NOT MY FIRST BRUSH WITH DEATH

However, the day I woke in the hospital was not my first brush with death. The year I was a junior in high school a pickup truck ran over me. I was riding a motorcycle. My leg got wrapped around the truck's axle, which dragged me more than 100 feet.

When I woke from a one-week coma, family members were by my bed. One of them stayed with me every day during my month-long hospital stay and for several months while I was at home recovering from two surgeries. I was never alone.

I missed a total of two months of my junior year of high school. After the Christmas break, I was able to return to school. My principal allowed me to enroll in three one-semester classes: economics, business law, and Missouri history. These were the most meaningful classes I'd ever taken. They showed me that I could blend social science classes into the world of business.

I attended Truman State University and majored in economic geography. I studied why corporations decided to locate in certain areas. For example, why is Boeing, an aircraft company, headquartered in Seattle, Washington, and not in southern California, which has better flying conditions?

While I'm still fascinated by geography, in college I discovered that I was also interested in people; why they decided to do what they did. So, after receiving an undergraduate degree, I earned a master's in counseling.

After college, Bank of America's consumer finance division (FinanceAmerica) offered me a job, which lasted 10 years. There, afraid of making a mistake or being fired, I quit three times. The first time I left, I took a year to study accounting.

I met Celia in an accounting class.

A high school government teacher, she was preparing to become a licensed stockbroker. Unlike me, Celia saw no limits to what she could do. Her encouragement and support helped me see that my strength at the bank (which hired me back all three times!) was helping customers develop a cash flow statement, so they could better make payments on past-due accounts. This realization helped me to understand my passion was to mentor people; my life mission was to help others be successful.

THE PERFECT PLACE

My next job was at a homeless shelter in downtown Dallas, where I taught a Life Skills class and offered career counseling. I also started working part-time in The Learning Center at Richland College, part of the Dallas County Community College District (DCCCD), where I tutored students in accounting.

Richland was the perfect place for me! Even though I was still shy and awkward in front of groups, I was good at mentoring students one-on-one. Eight years later, I accepted a full-time position in The Learning Center and was soon promoted to an assistant dean position. There I started a club which helped students access resources on the Richland campus, within the DCCCD, Dallas metroplex and state and federal governments.

Contributing to the success of students was rewarding, but I still felt that my skills were lacking. I just listened to people. Anyone could do that. I kept asking myself if I were not so shy, could I do more?

In September 2001 I attended my first circle of trust retreat sponsored by the Center for Renewal and Wholeness in Higher Education (CRWHE). From then until the fall of 2017, I participated in multiple retreats, even traveling to Pawleys Island, South Carolina, to sit in three circles. Those experiences began to change me radically.

The first few years I barely spoke. I preferred listening, a more comfortable role for a shy soul. Questions posed by the facilitators helped me claim my leadership style, one based on what Parker Palmer calls birthright gifts, or qualities and attributes we're born with. Slowly I started using the skills I named and learned in circles of trust with students. I asked more incisive questions, ones that helped them understand what their gifts were and how to set achievable goals.

THE TOUCHSTONES

Three of the Touchstones, with which we begin each retreat, were pivotal in the change which took place in my life. The first was to *presume welcome and welcome others into the space*. Welcome seemed foreign to me at first. But as I dove deeper into the work, I realized that if *I* felt welcome, then that *all of me* was welcome: the parts that had been a success and the parts of me that had failed. My shyness. My awkwardness. My fear of letting people get to know me. My vulnerability. In those circles, reflecting deeply on various life experiences, I realized that if I learned from my mistakes, I could chart a new path forward, one that could lead to wholeness.

The second touchstone I latched on to was *when things become difficult, turn to wonder*. Before circle work, when I was caught in a situation where I was embarrassed or made fun of, the fight or flight response kicked in, and I ran. Turning to wonder allowed me to stay present in a conversation and learn from another person's ideas, positions, and opinions. Relying on this practice, I forged several deep friendships that would have never happened in my previous life.

The third touchstone was *suspend judgment.* When I had the opportunity to talk with someone, of whatever gender, ethnicity, socio-economic status or nationality, I tried to find common ground. This guideline helped me widen my ability to see the whole person and understand there is something I can appreciate and admire within every person.

AFTER THE WRECK

Then the wreck that claimed the lives of Celia and Mary Jane upended my life. I left the hospital a broken man and had no choice but to let people see my vulnerability.

My healing from that traumatic event was made possible by the people and practices I'd come to know sitting in circles of trust. Colleagues who'd been in those circles with me became extended family.

- Dave Shorow picked me up from the hospital and drove me home.

- Ann Faulkner and her husband came an hour after I got home and returned each day for a week to help with paperwork, notify people, and plan Celia's funeral.

- Martha Timberlake, my boss and a CRWHE facilitator, sat in my office to help me acclimate back to work and to share in my grief.

- Sue Jones urged me to chronicle how circle of trust work helped me heal from my loss, and I began to glimpse the gifts.

I came to understand the importance of grief work in healing and wholeness. As I shared the grief work I'd done with

DCCCD employees, I began to see with more clarity the gifts that accompanied the tragedy.

The greatest of those gifts was Elaine Sullivan's introduction to Marilyn Herridge, mother of two grown children and three grandchildren. In 2018, we will have been married six years. Thanks to my work and my friends in circles of trust, I can truly embrace the gifts wrapped in grief.

John Millemon, Administrator Emeritus at Richland College, a campus of the Dallas County Community College District, is currently a facilitator with the Center for Renewal and Wholeness in Higher Education. He lives in Dallas, Texas, with his wife Marilyn Herridge. They enjoy travelling in the U.S. and abroad. He can be contacted through e-mail: jmill@dcccd.edu

Choose Life!

By Barbara Harris

I vividly recall the news that shattered our family: Mom has cancer. It was my sophomore year in high school when she headed from our home in northwest Florida to Oschner Hospital in New Orleans for her surgery. Mom received follow-up radiation and chemo treatments for her non-Hodgkins lymphoma, returning home dramatically changed. No longer the strong, sturdy 145-pound woman who spoke her mind without hesitation, now Mom was frail, hesitant and 20 pounds lighter, someone who fell headlong into a deep, dark depression. *Always in her pink bathrobe* and lying on the couch, Mom was afraid to be alone.

Looking back to my high school years through the lens of Courage and Renewal work, I can see the roots of what inspires my life and current work as a hospital chaplain. The invitation to share my story for this book has given me the chance to reflect on how this work and the writings of Parker Palmer have created the space for me to better understand my own story.

I realize that my journey began long before the day I met Elaine Sullivan from the Center for Renewal and Wholeness in Higher Education (CRWHE), long before I became a facilitator, long before I became editor of *Shape* Magazine, long before I became a hospital chaplain supporting patients in choosing life.

My journey begins with my mom's transformation. *No more pink bathrobe.* From seemingly out of nowhere, mom found her strength, her will to live. One day, mom decided to paint the inside of the whole house, and she became herself again. Fully alive, yet now in a fight for her life. Bravely, she faced adversity, especially the cancer that would recur again and again. Years later, she would laughingly remark, "I got my strength through painting."

Often at college, I would receive a call from her. "The darn thing's back," she'd say with a trace of frustration mixed with sure-fire determination to beat it. With hardly a breath in between, she would announce when her next chemo would be. This pattern repeated for years. Diagnosed at age 47, she lived to be 71. *Live she did.*

Reflecting back, I realize she taught me how to live. She had a purpose, one loud and clear. Her refrain: "I have to live for my children and grandchildren." I also learned from her that life was not a given, but a gift.

As my mother so bravely lived her life, what about me? Years later, as I became a CRWHE facilitator and was introduced to Parker Palmer's writings, his words about letting your life speak resonated with me. I learned the value of claiming birthright gifts through Courage and Renewal work. Claiming my gifts grounded me and allowed me to listen to my life speaking, rather than trying to tell my life what I wanted to do with it.

In *Let Your Life Speak,* Parker encourages looking for clues to birthright gifts by considering what you loved as a child. For reminders, I returned to a favorite childhood snapshot: my dad giving me my first ball and bat at age three. For years, he'd regularly play catch and hit ground balls to me in the front yard. My childhood red ball cap hangs on the back of my door as a tangible reminder. My adulthood love of sports, rock climbing, hiking and kayaking can be traced to climbing trees and romping endlessly through the woods, playing sports with my dad and brothers, the neighborhood kids and on school teams in childhood through college.

Looking back, it is clear that I was always encouraged by my parents to do what I love, to live according to my gifts. Thus, I studied physical education in college and taught and coached in my early career. Next, I pursued graduate studies in exercise physiology. While engaged in wellness work in the years following, a chance opportunity came my way that drew on my love of teaching and wellness work. Inviting me to take her job, the Editor–in-Chief of *Shape* magazine told me that my classroom would simply grow from about 30-40 to 650,000 (monthly readers). Over a dinner in Malibu in 1987, I said Yes to the job and the welcome relocation from Houston, Texas, to Los Angeles, and to all the possibilities of heading west.

With a passion for teaching and ensuring the integrity of the magazine's scientific information, my 15-plus years as Editor-in-Chief was a good fit. I engaged the whole staff in planning each issue, recognizing that good ideas could come from everyone. Each person on staff, art, editorial and administration, contributed during planning; everyone had a voice in the magazine and its mission: "To help women create better lives," mind, body and spirit.

During that time at the magazine, I met CRWHE facilitator, Elaine Sullivan, who introduced me to Parker's work. For years, I asked the question to *Shape* readers which emerged to me from reflecting on Parker's *Let Your Life Speak* and from the Courage and Renewal gatherings: *"Are you living the life that wants to live in you?"* Fascination with this question inspired the creation of Shape Your Life workshops for women in Washington, which included climbing Mt. Rainier, and in Costa Rica, which involved fitness, nutrition and spirituality sessions, along with hiking and class V river rafting.

I also met psychiatrist Carl Hammerschlag at a conference in Lake Louise, Canada. According to Carl, author of *The Dancing Healers*, he learned to practice medicine on a Hopi reservation when asked to dance at the bedside of a man who was ill. From the Hopi ways, Carl said he learned the fundamental role of community in healing. Canoeing with Carl out on Lake Louise, I remember his telling me, "You don't have to paddle your own canoe." The concept of sacred community emerged in a profound way for me that moment, and a day later, out hiking.

During a solitary hike up to the Lake Louise Tea House, my Roman Catholic spirituality profoundly expanded. Beyond the rhythmic awareness of my stepping, I sensed light brightly streaming through the birch trees, and the leaves dancing, shimmering. Everything around me became alive, and I felt at one with it all. "We are all one," the trees and the plants seemed to whisper.

Returning to the magazine transformed, I invited each staff member to take out a piece of paper to write about their purpose; not that they were a copy editor or writer, that was their job. *"What is your purpose? Why are you here (alive on earth)?"* I asked. Reflecting on my own purpose, I remember thinking, one day I will be a minister, somewhere, somehow.

That quest for purpose, for passion, for letting my life speak from the depths of who I am has driven me for years. So has what scholar of world myth Joseph Campbell describes as more important than the search for meaning in life. Seeking the ultimate, *the experience of being (or feeling fully) alive,* led me to high-altitude mountaineering, twice climbing Washington's Mt. Rainier, a 15,000+ foot mountain; Hunai Potosi in the Bolivian Andes and ringing in the new millennium atop Mt. Kilimanjaro in Africa; rock climbing 1,000+ feet up the East face of 14,000+ foot Mt. Whitney in California; and kayaking among the Vancouver islands off the coast of British Columbia, seeing Orca whales by day and the Northern Lights by night.

Then, about 15 years after my hike up to the Tea House in Lake Louise, I met the God I knew in my heart unexpectedly, when invited by my neighbors to attend a United Church of Christ congregation in Woodland Hills, California. The church's values, peace and social justice, open and affirming (welcoming LGBTQ), resonated with my own. With the support and blessing of the congregation, I was off to seminary in San Francisco. True to Parker's words of living with integrity and listening to my inner voice, I also completed integrative wellness studies and interfaith studies through other institutions, and was ordained through an interfaith seminary.

Parker's writings have informed my theological statement in seminary and current chaplaincy service. At work during health and illness, my view of the transcendent within is an ever-present luring into "a hidden wholeness," the focus of Parker's 2004 book.

Parker wrote in *A Hidden Wholeness* that wholeness means "embracing brokenness as part of life." Illness and loss may shatter one's sense of self. A patient can feel broken and diseased, disconnected from their wholeness and what was once meaningful (work and life as one knows it), like Melanie, a patient I met who had suffered a stroke ten years ago. "My life ended (with the stroke)," she said. Yet, illness and death are integral to the natural trajectory of life.

Salvation lay in patients reconnecting to this transcendent within and letting go, allowing ongoing transformation to occur. Another patient, Lois, who was leaving the hospital with a prognosis of months to live, said, "All my life, I have held my thoughts and feelings mostly inside. I have often been unavailable for birthdays or holiday family celebrations. Now, in this last chapter, I intend to learn new skills of being open and expressive, and new ways of being with my family." As a butterfly emerges from a chrysalis and the snake sheds its outer skin, the universal call throughout life is one of yielding to an ever-present healing, transformative mystery at work.

Through interfaith studies, I met my chaplaincy mentor, who would later guide me in doing inner shadow work while in sacred community with colleagues. Working with my shadow includes healing my family of origin issues, which are rooted in alcoholism and co-dependency. This includes healing patterns of deferring my own needs, stuffing feelings, and the tendency to "fix others."

Elaine Sullivan also became a lifelong mentor for me. For years, when navigating difficult times, I would call Elaine seeking advice. Holding fast to the CRWHE touchstone "no advice giving," Elaine would respond with questions to invite forth my inner voice.

Long before entering seminary, my most significant chaplaincy training was sitting with my mother in the hospital near her death in December, 1995. I remember her asking me, "Am I dying?"

I answered, "I don't know. Are you?" I knew that she knew better than me.

From the practice of Clearness Committees in my Courage and Renewal work, I have come to understand that true knowledge lies within each person, an awareness I aim for upon entering each patient's room in my current chaplaincy practice. As patients and families seek answers, I strive to provide what Quaker Douglas Steere describes in *On Listening to Another* as "holy listening," which is "to listen another's soul into...

disclosure and discovery," providing what Parker describes as a quiet inviting of the soul.

My fundamental role as a chaplain is to support patients in *choosing life*, or wellness, *regardless of prognosis*. Facing illness and death, we have the capacity to choose among many possibilities. Self-actualization doesn't end at the onset of illness, but is the work of a lifetime.

I like physician John Travis' Illness/Wellness Continuum: to the left is illness (defined by progressive sickness); to the right is progressive wellness. Yet, wellness is not a static state. Wellness involves caring for the whole self, including using the mind constructively, caring for the physical body, expressing emotions, being connected to others, and creatively involved in life. According to Travis in his *Wellness Workbook: How to Achieve Enduring Health and Vitality*, "what determines wellness is not so much one's place on the continuum; but 'the direction' *(toward illness or wellness)* one is facing."

Wellness is *choosing life*.

I apply this model with patients, such as Grace, who died after a seven-month odyssey with leukemia. Walking into Grace's hospital room, I regularly encountered family and friends. Grace would invite friends to sing and make crafts with her. Energy permitting, she also did some Zumba dancing there. During spiritual care visits, Grace spoke her dreams for herself and her family.

Grace did not just *choose life*, she inspired others to do so, to literally Praise Life, to jump in and make a splash! I offer this praise poem I wrote for Grace:

Amazing Grace

Praise Life!

You Zumba danced in your hospital room
  In between chemo treatments.

Praise Life!

Approaching life's end we took a walk,
    You dragging your IV pole
    Wearing your blue cotton hospital gown
    flowing behind you.

Praise Life!

You sang from your depths,
    Giving voice to what you will miss, what you
    long for,
        To see your son marry
        To know your daughter will
        Receive all she needs to flourish.

Praise Life!

You seek assurance that your Ernie will
        laugh and golf again.
            He's so sad.

Praise Life!

You seek to know if your swimming friends will
jump into the pool wildly again, and make a
splash when you are no longer here.

Praise Life!

Yes! They did. Upon the news of your death,
Holding hands at the water's edge,
The Splashers jumped in, fully clothed. Yes!

Praise Life!

Former *Shape* Editor-in-chief, Rev.
Barb Harris, MDiv, MA, is an ordained
interfaith minister, currently serving
as a hospital chaplain. She lives in the
northwest, where she enjoys kayaking and hiking and watching the
deer roam her neighborhood, especially in spring, when moms can
often be seen chasing their frolicking fawns. She can be contacted
via email, harris.barbara1@gmail.com

Much More than What is Obvious: The Healing Art of Poetry

By John Fox

The golden fleece exists: accept no lie.
Each of us is the golden fleece of our being.

Odysseas Elytis from *Open Papers*
(Translated by Olga Broumas & T. Begley)

I was living in a spiritual community, nestled in the foothills of the Sierra Nevada. By that time, I had lived there two years. I was 25. That Sunday afternoon January 26, 1981, I was sitting with a group of people in a cramped basement area of the publications building. In this place many things happened: a cassette tape library for all the meditation classes, housing for graphic artists for books being created. I was in charge of printing and mailing out the Yoga Correspondence Course, *14 Steps to Perfect Joy.* I used an ancient copying machine called a Gestetner Cyclograph.

A BREATH MADE OF BLISS

The exact circumstances surrounding this breath are kind of odd. About 16 people crowded into this small area, watching the San Francisco 49er's play the Cincinnati Bengals in Super Bowl XVI! I said it was "odd"—all these calm "yogis" watching that fascinating and brutal game.

Anandi Cornell, a significant teacher in this community, dedicated to the practice of Ashtanga Yoga, with an emphasis on devotion, sat directly behind me. At some point, she got up from her chair, and leaning slightly forward, while standing up,

Anandi's exhaled breath glanced against my skin.

When she breathed on my arm, I felt her breath was infused with bliss...

This was a remarkable sensation and perception—to feel someone's breath in this way, to read it in my heart and body as *knowing* her breath expressed a deep quality of energy, aliveness, joy, soul.

This happened in a moment. I took note of it—but I didn't say anything to Anandi. (Until I wrote about it to her last year.) What I did was I never forgot it. From the perspective of daily life, this could not have been more of a mundane and passing moment. Yet...

In this singular and beautiful moment I became aware of a heightened consciousness, and truly, the blessing of another human being without the slightest effort. This was not the first time I experienced something like this; yet, I begin my essay here, with this moment of a blissful breath, because it embodies what I will write about in sharing my story.

TRANSCENDENT

Since the age of 16, I wanted to learn about the experience of transcendence in its wide variety of expressions. When I became quiet and still, I could feel with certainty that other people, including myself, have and could experience that heightened consciousness/transcendence.

The transcendent drew me because I longed for whatever taste I could have of it; it fed me with Wonder and Beauty. It showed me something *more* than myself—and—with that certainty, I felt a sense of potential belonging.

However, I should say quickly that my "deep certainty" is still, and was then, weighted by a stark and more shadowed feeling of the incredibly elusive and seemingly rare nature of this experience. While that certainty is informed by clear hints of direct experience (the awareness that someone's breath shows bliss, etc.), I have spent much more time in my life feeling a *raw longing* for that larger experience of Wonder and Beauty, for an experience free of only my personality, free of my own pain, searching for an essence within myself that could open towards the Unknown.

THE UNKNOWN

Poetry is the single form of communication I have found which orients me within a field I recognize as being closer to the unknown. That writing poetry has affinity with the unknown is not surprising. Robert Frost said, "I have never started a poem yet whose end I knew. Writing a poem is discovering." True enough!

The Black Mountain and San Francisco poet Robert Duncan wrote these words in his lovely poem, *Often I Am Permitted to Return to a Meadow:*

> **as if were a scene made-up by the mind,**
> **that is not mine, but is a made-place,**
>
> **that is mine, it is so near the heart,**
> **an eternal pasture folded in all thought...**

--excerpted from his book, *The Opening of the Field*

Something alchemical happens in the poem when Duncan enters "a made-place." The poem itself *is* that made-place, created in the mind, and in *making a place*, that place all of a sudden becomes *"mine."* This imagined sacred meadow is created through the agency of poem-making.

But the hub-bub of daily life, our consumer culture (among

other things!) does not honor this creativity. It ignores, diminishes and/or disparages such sensitivity. At the very least, our iPhone-cluttered world does not slow down enough to feel this. I say we *can* slow down, I say we *can* take heart; John Keats' immortal words are meant to give you and me courage. They are also meant to secure a place for the treasure of the imagination:

> *I am certain of nothing but the holiness*
> *of the heart's affections and the truth of*
> *the imagination — what the imagination*
> *seizes as beauty must be truth — whether*
> *it existed before or not.*

> --John Keats' letter to Benjamin Bailey,
> 22 Nov 1817

I turn often to this eternal and radical statement. Valuing my heart's affection and imagination were part of my life from those teen years on. Because of poetry, I practiced getting to know those affections, and with my own voice, I committed myself to express that imaginative truth—in my own unique way.

Two major strands wove themselves together in my writing – beauty and suffering. My search for and recognition of beauty. My life and how living it brought suffering. I let both capture my full attention. The good fortune is that in addition to this, poetry opened up a window that showed me more-than-myself. THIS window of more-than-myself became the horizon place of transcendence.

BEING OPEN TO THE PRESENCE OF OTHERS

At the age of 23 I was living in Cleveland, Ohio, where I grew up. I had just graduated from Bard College. Returning home, I landed a job working at Cleveland Clinic Hospital. I didn't own a car. I didn't even drive. I got to work riding a city bus. And there, riding to work, I received the following poem:

A Place that Is Not a Place, Only Is
(while riding on the Cleveland bus, #9 Downtown)

"There is another world, but it is in this one."
W. B. Yeats

This bus is a place
that is not a place, only is —
moving us here together in an everyday occurrence.
I think of unpublished books,
unopened books,
unwritten scriptures; unspoken gospels,
I think of all these people
who I am with. The old person struggling
up the steps and the
young one clambering down.
I begin to wonder about a place that
is not a place, only is —
as the earliest dream or oldest memory.
Like flakes of snow drifting
over the very distinct footprints,
footprints of an old person
walking, an old woman bundled
in a warm woolen coat
gotten from the loom in a city of wisdom;
not of this time.
The old woman, glimpsed so briefly,
there being little in her mind
to attract attention to her solemnity:
seen through a space in snow-time

in the grace of many wrinkles
found in winter's face,
and in the days of slow travel and transport.
Days, I imagine where God
and loved ones and where one is living
had more of the thought and heart.
I wonder again about a place that is not a place,
only is —
as sunlight and wind through meadow grass
so wavelike, single and seamless
as a summer day can be for only a child
with all motor cortex connections
unrestrained and dateless,
living in what is called
the movement of the Holy Spirit.
Suddenly to discover being one with,
this child finds summerhouse, waterway,
tree, blue sky and meadow grass more than enough
to speak about, to show and share
with many angels, delighted
to listen, to see the sounds
of child's voice, dance of child's feet,
rest of child's body laid down
in meadow grass, joyous feeling
scattering away to the sun at horizon.
Horizons! The unseen stars
in the very first sky,
deep in the natural afternoon:
are still, very still, in a place
that is not a place, only is.

Each person who rode the #9 bus down Euclid Avenue had their own, individual life of heartbreak and everyday joy. That, too, is worthy of poetry. Yet, with my imagination, I was paying attention to something else – to that elder woman, to that child; imagining something close to what Yeats had to say about another world being embedded in this one. By finding words for it – words imbued with metaphor, image and all the elements that poetry offers, I imagined and made something I could both share with others and call my own.

I believed then and now that we are each much more than what is obvious.

A WINDOW TO THE UNKNOWN AND ALSO THE TRUE

In the 1980's I became aware of the poetry and thought of the Greek poet, Odysseas Elytis. Elytis won the Nobel Prize for Literature in 1979. He wrote continuously, in a variety of ways, about the same thing – claiming for people and life itself, a deep and beautiful heritage. I found this thrilling and confirmative.

The Golden Fleece represents divine sovereignty, a shining, precious spirit of royalty for each person, whose very reality puts death on notice. Elytis speaks to this in a very compelling way in *Open Papers: Selected Essays*:

> *The golden fleece exists: accept no lie. Each of us is the golden fleece of our being. Death doesn't keep us from seeing and recognizing it; that is a hoax. We must empty death of all it's been stuffed with and bring it to absolute clarity, so that the real mountains and real grass are seen in it, the maligned world brimming with dew more luminous than any precious tears.*

That is what I await each year, one more
wrinkle on my brow, one less in my soul:
complete reversal, absolute transparence.

I wrote because poetry begins from
the point where the last word does not
belong to death

(translated by Olga Broumas and T. Begley)

Surprisingly, his transcendent poetry gave me practical inspiration for living in this world, on this earth, in my actual life. The time I met this great poet's work was the precise time I was deciding to learn how to run again—after the amputation of my right leg below the knee in 1974—a very real challenge!

Elytis' words spoke to me:

. . .My friend, when night wakens your electric grief
I see the tree of the heart spreading
Your arms open beneath a pure idea
To which you call
But which will not descend
For years and years:
It up there and you down here.

And yet longing's vision awakens flesh one day

--excerpt from *With what stones, what blood and what iron,*
Selected Poems, translation by Edmund Keeley & Philip Sherard

I cannot overemphasize the catalytic power of these lines, this image. No one had ever described phantom pain so accurately: *electric grief.* This poem reminded me that the whole of who I am is alive in a much bigger space than only my body. That I am connected to—my arms can open to and call upon—that "pure idea." And then, to be called *friend* by the poet! This whole poem lit an inner fire that gave me direction, hope and power.

Eventually I ran a marathon and other long distances and with this, my awakened flesh started to sing. It is not that the phantom pain disappeared; rather, I had discovered an uplifting and connecting reality within myself. I wrote Elytis to thank him. I sent a handful of my own poems, including this one:

WHEN JEWELS SING

Radiance results from earth's pressure:
with each moment's precision,
life works us into clear-cut uniqueness.

A community of precious human beings
with origins primitive and wild as diamonds,
faceted by skilled and invisible hands that turn us
upon a wheel dusted with God's bright dark silence,
we become men and women joined to walk
swarthy, holy, original and transparent.

Catching first light of day upon ourselves,
our voices sing of truth and loveliness
in response to vows first sung by stars.

In May of 1987 he replied from Athens:

"A window has been opened for you
towards the world of the unknown but
also the true and it will help you."

It is astonishing to consider this: *what is unknown knows me.* I feel greatly encouraged to know this: *the unknown will help me.* His simple words profoundly affect my relationship to the transcendent. Like the statement of John Keats, this sentence points in the direction of creativity and its relationship to the transcendent.

I want to pause from this discussion of transcendence and the unknown—and give you food for thought about how important it is and how possible it is to attend your own meadow-of-imagination-near-the-heart through the healing art of poem-making.

A SPECIAL PERSON OR FINDING WHAT YOU DIDN'T LOSE?

We may think one needs to be a special person or is otherwise designated (from on high?) to carry this role as a poet. As you must know, I take great exception to this view.

A two-and-a-half-year-old boy named Ian looks out a car window and exclaims to his mother, "Look, Mom, the clouds... they are like mashed potatoes!"

Ian did not ask anyone's permission to make and express such a delightful connection. He trusted his enthusiasm and shared his spontaneous insight. Ian had not taken a class in the making of simile! This story demonstrates a clear, even miraculous sign, that there is a creative and imaginative spark in each person.

It has been my lifelong calling to make a place where you, dear reader, can get in touch with that spark and realize that the writing of your own words is going to provide a huge step of inspired self-empowerment. It helps to make a fertile place for self-expression.

This is, as I understand it, the purpose of "third things" in the CRWHE work, grounded in Parker Palmer's writing. Introducing thoughtfully chosen poems and reading them out loud together is a way to take this further, to initiate writing, your own writing that is meaningful and generative, that matters.

Further, sharing your writing with others who are open-hearted and non-judgmental is an equally strong step towards weaving a fresh spirit of community. Perhaps this is *a fourth thing.*

However, rather than taking the risk to find our own words, we lean towards valuing the words of others. We respect consciousness leaders because we think they are eloquent and wise. And perhaps they **are** eloquent and wise. It is not a criticism of valuing others whom we perceive as wise and eloquent—but too often, in the process, I believe we cede our creative potential to those people we greatly respect.

That respected person could be Parker Palmer. It could be John Fox. It could be that holy woman Hildegard of Bingen and that ecstatic poet Jalal ad-Din Rumi. You name him or her. How about this—it could be *you.*

My faith in human beings says this: our creativity comes naturally and it is necessary to further our deeper growth. It is also necessary if we are to know one another in truer ways, as William Stafford writes in *A Ritual to Read to Each Other:*

> *If you don't know the kind of person I am*
> *and I don't know the kind of person you are*
> *a pattern that others made may prevail in the world*
> *and following the wrong god home we may miss our star.*

I acknowledge there may be risk involved, there may be a time of struggle and it may require courage to get going. To encourage and ease your way I offer support in my book, *Finding What You Didn't Lose: Expressing Your Truth and Creativity Through Poem-Making.* You can start anywhere and all on your own. Write down favorite words (about a dozen, include some verbs) and then shape those words into a poem. You are welcome to play.

This essay emphasizes my deep attraction to what I describe as the transcendent nature of Wonder and Beauty; yet, it may surprise you to know that I feel ambivalence about it. You may wonder why, until now as I offer this last poem *Home Equity,* I haven't mentioned God once or even used that word:

HOME EQUITY

God's hands over my head —
that's what a roof means!
But when I wake up in Spring light,
The only thing of worth is an open door.

Another source of ambivalence!

My ambivalence comes from the fact that I am leaving out the fact that my involvement and care for issues of social justice and politics, my personal life and work, my disillusionments with religion(s) and even a love for classical music and baseball —all of these capture my attention too, almost as much as everything I have written here.

At times it feels like my real calling to grow and thrive is found in this world with all of its suffering and inconsistencies, its shadows and tangled roots.

Home Equity suggests that simply by being lucky enough at this time to have a roof over my head, I am aware of some protection from God. Then this awareness comes in contact with the arrival of "Spring" that there is something beyond any concept of God. (My ambivalence: how about all of those millions of people who have no roof over their head?!)

Perhaps in responding to this invitation made by my friend Elaine Sullivan to share my story, perhaps as I enter into probably the last quarter of my life, writing to you of this love for that "beyond," I am being made aware that this call felt at 16 years old, asks for rekindling.

Perhaps the only real question might be: What is *my* breath made of these days?

John Fox, CPT, is the founder and president of the Institute for Poetic Medicine. John has taught at the Institute for Transpersonal Psychology, John F. Kennedy University, California Institute of Integral Studies and Holy Names University. John has introduced the field of poetry therapy to professionals in education, cancer support, spiritual/pastoral care, counseling, and arts-in-medicine. He has worked with people throughout America as well as in the United Kingdom, Ireland, Israel, Canada, South Korea and Kuwait. He is the author of *Finding What You Didn't Lose* and *Poetic Medicine*. He is past president of the National Association for Poetry Therapy. He can be reached at http://www.poeticmedicine.org/ and you can learn a bit more about John's Institute of Poeticx Medicine in the final section of this book.

Were We Wrong?

By RubyRenee Wood

She was born a quiet baby, to a family of boisterous
talk-a-lots. From birth on, her smile was powerful,
thought dissolving to the viewer. When anyone asked,
"doesn't she talk?" her gaze remained constant,
conveying peace, so the person would pause, smile
back, and having forgotten their question move on.
The doctors said she probably thought in pictures,
was incapable of translating into spoken or written
words. As she aged, she painted huge watercolors
full of fleshy colors with odd facial features that
went unrecognized until after her passing. Close-ups
of things like eyebrows, pores or moles, nostrils, an
earlobe. Her youngest niece, Sylvie, discovered the
subject matter. Blithely walking from painting to
painting, she named off the contents of each piece.
"That's Grampy's hairy mole, that one's the dark holes
on Jeffrey's nose, that's my mama's ear." And so on,
until the entire family was muted like our dead relative.
She'd truly looked at us. I would like to know more.
Were they the observations of a simple mind or the
expression of a mind exceeding any of ours? Her smile
became all we expected. Were we wrong?

**RubyRenee Wood supports the arts as an Office Assistant to the
Carlsen Center Performing Arts Series General Manager at Johnson
County Community College. She lives in Kansas City, Missouri,
where she pursues any and every type of creative expression with
her darling husband CHVCK and cat Blanche. She can be contacted
through e-mail: RubyRenee44@gmail.com**

The Third Mandala

Wholeness as a Way of Being

The Movement Way

By Parker J. Palmer

I often say that if my ideas never left the pages of my books, they wouldn't be of much use. I celebrate the people who put wheels on those ideas, who find ways to live with integrity, to take their inner work into the outer world.

The Writers in this book have done just that. They share individual stories of deciding to live divided no more and finding support through the Center for Renewal and Wholeness in Higher Education (CRWHE). I offer this look at the way of the movement, as a way to gain insight into what sustained them as they took the journey to the undivided life.

I began to understand movements when I saw the simple fact that nothing would ever have changed if reformers had allowed themselves to be done in by organizational resistance. Many of us experience such resistance as checkmate to our hopes for change. But for a movement, resistance is merely the place where things begin. The movement mentality, far from being defeated by organizational resistance, takes energy from opposition. Opposition validates the audacious idea that change must come.

The black liberation movement and the women's movement would have died aborning if racist and sexist organizations had been allowed to define the rules of engagement. But for some blacks, and for some women, that resistance affirmed and energized the struggle. In both movements, advocates of change found sources of countervailing power outside of organizational structures, and they nurtured that power in ways that eventually gave them leverage on organizations.

The genius of movements is paradoxical: they abandon the logic of organizations in order to gather the power necessary to rewrite the logic of organizations. Both the black movement and the women's movement grew outside of organizational boundaries—but both returned to change the lay, and the law, of the land.

How does a movement unfold and progress? I see four definable stages in the movements I have studied—stages that do not unfold as neatly as this list suggests, but often overlap and circle back on each other:

- Isolated individuals decide to stop leading "divided lives."

- These people discover each other and form groups for mutual support.

- Empowered by community, they take the risk to "go public."

- Alternative rewards emerge to sustain the movement's vision, which may force the conventional reward system to change.

STAGE ONE:
Choosing Integrity

The first stage in a movement can be described with some precision, I think. It happens when isolated individuals make an inner choice to stop leading "divided lives." Most of us know from experience what a divided life is. Inwardly we feel one sort of imperative for our lives, but outwardly we respond to quite another. This is the human condition, of course; our inner and outer worlds will never be in perfect harmony. But there are extremes of dividedness that become intolerable, and when the tension snaps inside of this person, then that person, and then another, a movement may be underway.

The decision to stop leading a divided life, made by enough people over a period of time, may eventually have political impact. But at the outset, it is a deeply personal decision, taken for the sake of personal integrity and wholeness. I call it the "Rosa Parks decision" in honor of the woman who decided, one hot Alabama day in 1955, that she finally would sit at the front of the bus.

Rosa Parks' decision was neither random nor taken in isolation. She served as secretary for the local NAACP, had studied social change at the Highlander Folk School, and was aware of others' hopes to organize a bus boycott. But her motive that day in Montgomery was not to spark the modern civil rights movement. Years later, she explained her decision with a simple but powerful image of personal wholeness: "I sat down because my feet were tired."

I suspect we can say even more: Rosa Parks sat at the front of the bus because her soul was tired of the vast, demoralizing gap between knowing herself as fully human and collaborating with a system that denied her humanity. The decision to stop leading a divided life is less a strategy for altering other people's values than an uprising of the elemental need for one's own values to come to the fore. The power of a movement lies less in attacking some enemy's untruth than in naming and claiming a truth of one's own.

There is immense energy for change in such inward decisions as they leap from one person to another and outward to the society. With these decisions, individuals may set in motion a process that creates change from the inside out. There is an irony here: We often think of movements as "confrontational," as hammering away at social structures until the sinners inside repent and we contrast them (often invidiously) with the "slow, steady, faithful" process of working for change from within the organization. In truth, people who take an organizational approach to problems often become obsessed with their unyielding "enemies," while people who adopt a movement approach must begin by changing themselves. These people have seized the personal insight from which all movements begin: No punishment can possibly be more severe than the punishment that comes from conspiring in the denial of one's own integrity.

STAGE TWO:
Communities of Encouragement and Support

But the personal decision to stop leading a divided life is a frail reed. All around us, dividedness is presented as the sensible, even responsible, way to live. So the second stage in a movement happens when people who have been making these decisions start to discover each other and enter into relations of mutual encouragement and support. These groups, which are characteristic of every movement I know about, perform the crucial function of helping the Rosa Parks of the world know that even though they are out of step, they are not crazy. Together we learn that behaving normally is sometimes nuts but seeking integrity is always sane. But it is clear from all great movements that mutual support is vital if the inner decision is to be sustained and if the movement is to take its next crucial steps toward gathering power.

STAGE THREE:
Going Public

The third stage of a movement has already been implied. As support groups develop, individuals learn to translate their private concerns into public issues, and they grow in their ability to give voice to these issues in public and compelling ways. To put it more precisely, support groups help people discover that their problems are not "private" at all but have been occasioned by public conditions and therefore require public remedies.

This has been the story of the women's movement (and of the black liberation movement as well). For a long time, women were "kept in their place" partly by a psychology that relegated the pain women felt to the private realm-grist for the therapeutic mill. But when women came together and began discovering the prevalence of their pain, they also began discerning its public roots. Then they moved from Freud to feminism.

The translation of private pain into public issues that occurs in support groups goes far beyond the analysis of issues; it also empowers people to take those issues into public places. It was in small groups (notably, in churches) that blacks were empowered to take their protest to the larger community in songs and sermons and speeches, in pickets and in marches, in open letters and essays and books. Group support encourages people to risk the public exposure of insights that had earlier seemed far too fragile for that rough-and-tumble realm.

I am using the word "public" here in a way that is more classical than contemporary. The public realm I have in mind is not the realm of politics, which would return us to the manipulation of organizational power. Instead, to "go public" is to enter one's convictions into the mix of communal discourse. It is to project one's ideas so that others can hear them, respond to them, and be influenced by them and so that one's ideas can be tested and refined in the public crucible. The public, understood as a vehicle of discourse, is pre-political. It is that primitive process of communal conversation, conflict, and consensus on which the health of institutionalized power depends.

The Writers in this book are taking a step towards going public by sharing their stories. Because this activity does not always have direct political impact, some skeptics may call it "mere words." But this criticism comes from an organizational mentality. By giving public voice to our stories, by naming and claiming alternative values, we can create something more fundamental than political change. We can create cultural change.

STAGE FOUR:
Alternative Rewards

As a movement passes through the first three stages, it develops ways of rewarding people for sustaining the movement itself. In part, these rewards are simply integral to the nature of each stage; they are the rewards that come from living one's values, from belonging to a community, from finding a public voice. But in stage four, a more systematic pattern of alternative rewards emerges, and with it comes the capacity to challenge the dominance of existing organizations.

The power of organizations depends on their ability to reward people who abide by their norms, even the people who suffer from those norms. A racist society depends on a majority who are rewarded for keeping the minority "in its place" and on a minority willing to stay there. But as members of either group discover rewards for alternative behavior, it becomes more difficult for racism to reign. An educational system that ignores human need in favor of a narrow version of professionalism depends on a reward system that keeps both faculty and students in their place. But as soon as rewards for alternative behavior emerge for either group, it becomes more difficult for reform to be denied its day.

What are the alternative rewards offered by a growing movement? As a movement grows, the meaning one does not find in conventional work is found in the meaning of the movement. As a movement grows, the affirmation one does not receive from organizational colleagues is received from movement friends. As a movement grows, careers that no longer satisfy may be revisioned in forms and images that the movement has inspired. As a movement grows, the paid work one cannot find in conventional organizations may be found in the movement itself.

In stage one, people who decide to live "divided no more" find the courage to face punishment by realizing that there is no punishment worse than conspiring in a denial of one's own integrity. That axiom, inverted, shows how alternative rewards can create cracks in the conventional reward system and then grow in the cracks: people start realizing there is no reward greater than living in a way that honors one's own integrity. Taken together, the two axioms trace a powerful vector of a movement's growth from rejecting conventional punishments to embracing alternative rewards.

These alternative rewards may seem frail and vulnerable when compared to the raises and promotions organizations are able to bestow upon their loyalists. So they are.

Integrity, as the cynics say, does not put bread on the table. But people who are drawn into a movement generally find that stockpiling bread is not the main issue for them. They have the bread they need and, given that, they learn the wisdom of another saying: "People do not live on bread alone."

We live, ultimately, on our integrity.

UNDERSTANDING THE MOVEMENT WAY

By understanding the stages of a movement, I hope we may see more clearly that many of us are engaged in a movement today, that we hold in our hands a form of power that has driven real change in recent times. At every stage of a movement there is both power to help change happen and encouragement for disheartened souls. Wherever we are on this journey, a step taken to renew our spirits may turn out to be a step towards wholeness, towards integrity—once we understand the movement way.

Parker J. Palmer is a writer, teacher and activist who works independently on issues in education, community, leadership, spirituality, and social change. Founder and Senior Partner of the Center for Courage & Renewal, he has authored 11 books, including *The Courage to Teach, Let Your Life Speak, A Hidden Wholeness, Healing the Heart of Democracy*, and most recently, *On the Brink of Everything: Grace, Gravity & Getting Old*. He holds a Ph.D. in sociology from the University of California at Berkeley, and his work has been recognized with 13 honorary doctorates and the William Rainey Harper Award, whose previous recipients include Margaret Mead, Elie Wiesel, Paolo Freire.

Two Streams, One Movement

By Estrus Tucker

My ongoing journey of living divided no more, that is my journey to sustain a truer alignment of my values and intentions with my daily attitude and actions, continues to wind around and through a diversity of structures, processes and systems. And with over 35 years of executive leadership experience in both operations and governance in the nonprofit sector, I have a ripe, relevant and growing collection of practices, strategies and stories to adapt and engage.

One of many great ironies of my journey is that in the midst of ever increasing demands for new, sophisticated and often intellectualized approaches and processes, it is the simpler person-centered practices leading to relational trust and friendship that facilitate and sustain meaningful change. Relational trust and friendship are critical human and social capital too often missing or minimized in our efforts to transform structures and systems.

My path has also been uniquely privileged to collaborate, serve and learn with gifted leaders from the Center for Renewal and Wholeness in Higher Education (CRWHE) and the Center for Courage & Renewal (CCR) for a great many years. Both organizations have been led by practitioners of principles and practices informed by the teaching and writing of Parker J. Palmer: principles and practices that appreciate the character of leadership born of the identity and integrity of the person within the role.

In many ways both organizations are branches of a single family tree, two streams in one movement in service of human wholeness and renewal.

As a CCR facilitator residing in Fort Worth, Texas, I have supported the CRWHE facilitator preparation and gatherings and experienced an inspiring alignment with the values and intentions that I have come to trust, embody and employ. These values and intentions are held not only in our shared language but in our hearts and the bonds of friendships that go beyond organizational structures and processes.

We live in communities, a nation and world where the demands for diversity, inclusion and equity are rightfully rising in the midst of political partisanship, institutional disruptions and conflict. We witness daily the ongoing personal and organizational trauma of key professionals struggling to sustain practices that resource their leadership and renew their selfhood. The often heralded and valiant efforts of individuals and stand-alone organizations are important and insufficient to transform larger communities of people and systems. We need a movement.

Movements are more about people than processes and structures. Movements at their best connect the longings of people with hopeful outcomes without compromising their respect and dignity.

Parker Palmer describes four provocative phases in his Movement Model:

1. The Decision to Live Divided No More

2. The Formation of Communities of Congruence

3. The Process of Going Public

4. The Emergence of Alternative Rewards

In the second phase, Communities of Congruence, he says, "As people start living undivided lives, they discover others who are on the same path, and come together in communities that offer three forms of support: (1) sustaining their sanity in a culture that regards the divided life as safe and sane; (2) practicing a private and fragile language of identity, integrity and meaning until it becomes muscular enough to enter the public realm; (3) developing skills and disciplines of social change that help people implement the heart's imperatives in the external world."

Our commitment to live undivided is reinforced and resourced in a community of congruence; reinforced to prepare us to engage, revise, expand and wisely discard old structures and processes and resourced to go public in new ways that reflect a movement scale. Beyond the structures of systems and organizations, people who commit to living divided no more are kindred advocates in honoring the human soul and creating spaces for our common humanity.

The Center for Renewal and Wholeness in Higher Education and the Center for Courage & Renewal are two of the streams among many now at a critical time demanding confluence in this vital movement of human wholeness and renewal.

Estrus Tucker served as the interim Executive Director of the Center for Courage & Renewal in 2018. For 20 years he has also served as a national Independent Consultant, Coach & Master Facilitator and is currently the principal consultant with the City of Worth's Race and Culture Initiative. He is a Vietnam-era Veteran, an ordained minister and an alumnus of UT at Arlington and the John Ben Shepherd Texas Public Leadership Forum, and the 2012 recipient of the International Association of Human Rights Agencies Individual Achievement Award for his leadership in facilitating transformational leadership in Mississippi; Belfast, Northern Ireland; Capetown, South Africa and Texas. Estrus resides in Lake Como, a historic African American Community in Fort Worth, Texas and can be reached at estrus@couragerenewal.org

Taking My Inner Work into the Outer World

By Sue Jones

The first time I heard Parker J. Palmer talk about formation, it struck a chord deep within me:

> *"Formation is journeying, individually and in community, to our inner selves, our hearts and souls, to identify our true selves and our deep integrity. From this center proceeds our action."*

In late summer of 1997, a group of us from the Dallas area went to Fetzer Institute's *Seasons* retreat center to meet Palmer and learn about his work. For me it was a life-altering experience.

Out of that encounter came the Center for Formation in the Community College (CFCC) with generous support from the Fetzer Institute, the Dallas County Community College District, and the League for Innovation in the Community College. We were fortunate to have strong support from the chair of our Board of Trustees, the Chancellor, and a Vice-Chancellor, as well as the president of Richland College, Steve Mittelstet.

Ann Faulkner and I were the founding co-directors, working closely with Earlene Bond, our executive administrative assistant. The Center's doors opened on March 5, 2001; Elaine Sullivan joined our team in the fall of 2002. Parker himself prepared Ann, Elaine and me in this work, with the help of the pilot facilitators he had already prepared. Marianne Houston mentored Ann and me (and I still hear her voice today!), and Elaine was mentored by Marcy Jackson, a founding co-director of the Center for Teacher Formation (CTF).

From the beginning, the CTF (now the Center for Courage

& Renewal) accepted individuals into facilitator preparation to work with K-12 teachers, and CFCC accepted teams nominated by community college leaders to bring the work back to their campuses. Our early experience taught us that a team of people—those who would be responsible for facilities and catering, those who handled marketing and advertising, and those who actually convened the circle and held the safe space—would be an extremely important model. We also recognized the importance of building relational trust among the team members as we prepared each of them in the work of formation and renewal and wholeness.

EXPANDING THE WORK

Several years after writing *The Courage to Teach*, Parker authored *A Hidden Wholeness*, and both centers expanded their work from teachers to a cross-professional population, and expanded their language from formation to circles of trust and courage and renewal work. We became the Center for Renewal and Wholeness in Higher Education, accepting not only community college faculty, but including higher education faculty as well as others who influenced student learning—librarians, tutors, student services personnel, and many others. Today we have expanded our facilitator preparation to include individuals from many other professions, such as spiritual direction, hospital chaplaincy, and business and industry; we have welcomed all of them with an open heart. Our annual Gathering reflects this diversity, when facilitators and facilitators-in-preparation from around the country gather in Texas to continue deepening our practice in renewal and wholeness and spending time in the joy of being together.

I have found this work to be so richly rewarding, a way of reconnecting my own soul and role. It is a privilege to witness an individual make the decision to live an authentic life, to refuse to live behind a façade that she or he has created and no longer needs. I have learned much about the paradox of the individual and the community, as only an individual can make this decision to live with integrity – and yet these changes often come with great conflict at home and/or work; without the presence of a knowledgeable and supportive community, the decision to live "divided no more" is often too hard to do alone.

Sometimes I have seen the power of our work in breathtaking terms. Following a 24-hour weekend retreat that I facilitated for a college in Maryland, a science professor went back to campus on Monday morning and sent to the group the first poem that she had ever written. She had found the courage, in her vulnerability as a new poet, to go public, after being in the retreat with what Parker calls a community of congruence in his Movement Model.

CRWHE has now prepared over 200 facilitators, and we hear from them many stories of similar experiences from individuals in their retreats. One of the most powerful observations is that people have felt safe to reveal their *light* **and** their *shadow* in a circle with others from their college or professional group because of the Touchstones, trusting that this information will be held with confidentiality. We set the bar high, and participants live up to expectations time and time again.

MY PERSONAL JOURNEY

My own journey has been one of both highs and lows.

Learning from Parker's writing and speaking has inspired me. I have learned about fear in education: those big, muscle-bound guys in my weight training class who seemed to discount me may really have feared that they might learn something from me. Administrators even have fears! And I have confronted my own fears as a teacher. I have been fortunate to be in a formation circle where I could express my fear without being afraid of being "fixed or set right" by members of the group.

I also have learned about the importance of the work-before-the-work and how to create space in my daily schedule for that. This is work in preparation for the work that I am about to do. Whereas I had been accustomed to going to my office and setting down my books and papers for one class and picking up those for the next class or meeting and going out the door, I now sit in my office and take time to do deep breathing and visualizing the student or colleague I would see next. This preparation has made such a difference in how calm I feel when I walk into the room, and, I believe, I am a better teacher or committee person because of it.

CREATING SPACE FOR MY OWN SOUL

Through the years I have not only had the opportunity to work with many groups, but also to go deeply into my own soul, my light and shadow. As a facilitator, I am also able to be a participant (this is an important practice in our work). I have been the focus person in a number of Clearness Committees where committee members held space for me to struggle with a problem or issue and to gain insight in a way that I would never have done on my own. The value of the Clearness Committee, in my experience, is that, whether I am a focus person or a committee member, I find clearness. The practice of open, honest questions and no fixing provides an amazingly safe space in which I can hear myself.

I have had the opportunity to talk about experiences of childhood and adolescence that I think formed who I became as a young adult and beyond. We lived in a suburb of Detroit, Michigan, for a few years during my late childhood, and one important childhood memory involved going to the Detroit

Tigers games. My mom was an avid baseball fan (I was born in October and she was listening to the World Series on the radio while she was in labor with me!); on Ladies' Days for the Tigers, females were admitted to the park for $1.00. My mom would load up our station wagon with my friends and me and off we would go to the game! Tiger Stadium was located in an area of poverty; driving to and from the games, I would see poor people, mostly African Americans, living in deplorable conditions. I remember feeling appalled that people actually lived in buildings that were crumbling; many had no sidewalk or porch to protect them from the street traffic.

Even as a young child, I felt something was so wrong, as off we would go to our suburban home and all its niceties, while the people I saw near Tiger Stadium were probably wondering from where their next meal would come.My family had moved from Lincoln, Nebraska, to the Detroit area because my father, who worked for Goodyear Tire and Rubber Company, was transferred to Detroit in a new position.

When I was in the 7th grade my dad was transferred back to Nebraska. Apparently his job in Michigan, which included some sales and business lunches, became too stressful for him, and he started having a cocktail at lunch with the other (mostly) men. One thing led to another and he was soon in full-blown alcoholism. He was fortunate in that Goodyear did not fire him but changed his position back to a research chemist. Unfortunately, he was unable to stop drinking even with his return to Nebraska. I had no knowledge of my father's alcoholism because, until that time, he was not drinking.

The summer after I graduated from high school, our Spanish teacher and a history teacher loaded a group of us into a Greyhound bus, and we headed from Nebraska to Mexico. Here was another eye-opening experience! I saw people plowing fields with oxen and wooden yokes and others living in actual cardboard lean-tos. As we were entering Mexico City in the early evening, I saw two men kicking another who was lying in the gutter of the street. Again I felt indignant and helpless, as my younger self had felt traveling to Tiger Stadium. Why weren't we doing more to help these people improve their living conditions and thus their lives? What could we do? What could **I** do? I decried the conditions that I saw.

FALLING INTO A HOLE

I felt as though a big hole opened up and I just fell into it. My usual sense of firm footing in the world was lost. Through some excellent therapy, and later through Clearness Committees, I owned my need to have control so that I wouldn't ever be blindsided again. As I came to the understanding that sometimes control is needed, but often it is not, I was able to give up being "right" and usually just went with the flow. Acknowledging my shadow for a need to control helped me to let go and not always inflict my control needs on others.

Also through the Clearness process in those later years later, I realized one of my birthright gifts is a sense of justice and fairness. I had felt so defeated and helpless by what I had observed in Detroit and Mexico while those around me (friends and classmates) seemed to ignore what they saw or to be unmoved by it. Now I was able to find ways to name and use those gifts.

Though occasionally knocked off balance, I feel now that I am living my life on the Möbius strip, with a sense of seamlessness between my inner life and the outer world. Derek Walcott's poem, *Love After Love*, is one I often return to for solace and inspiration. I especially love the lines:

You will love again
the stranger who was yourself.

... Give back your heart
to itself, to the stranger who has loved you
all your life...

This work has allowed me to know myself, the stranger who really was me, and to be able to give back my heart to myself. I never imagined that I could take my own inner life—with all the shadows and warts as well as the strengths and gifts—into my outer world and have such inspiring work, the work toward renewal and wholeness for myself and others.

Dr. Sue Jones is professor emerita at the Dallas County Community College District and the Director of CRWHE at Richland College (crwhe@dcccd. edu). She continues to find the work of renewal and wholeness to be the richest work she has had the opportunity to do. Sue lives with her husband, David Klundt, and their two dogs. She is thrilled to be Mimi to seven wonderful grandchildren. She may be reached at sjones@dcccd.edu

All People. All Voices. All Matter.
Valencia College's Peace and Justice Institute

By Rachel C. Allen

The Peace and Justice Institute (PJI) at Valencia College in Orlando, Florida, which began with individuals and has impacted the lives of more than 25,000 people on campus and in the community, is a living example of Parker J. Palmer's Movement Model. The story of how Palmer's four stages unfolded on our college campus begins with individuals, including me, who awakened to self and came together to decide how we wanted to show up in the world.

FIRST STAGE: CHOOSING INTEGRITY

My decision to stop leading a divided life grew out of personal recovery in a 12-step program. In recovery, I learned the lesson Parker teaches so well: *I cannot lead others to a place I have not been myself.* I'd been interested in peace and justice issues all my life, and as a result of working the 12 steps, became empowered to bring my interest to the forefront at the college. To work for peace and justice meant I had to be the peace I wanted to see in the world. I could not pass on to a student, colleague, or friend something I did not possess. I could not teach peace, love, or community building until I embodied peace, love and community. I could not give respect until I respected myself.

Personal integrity requires us to be the same person on the inside that we appear to be on the outside. We often have to release the masks we wear as teachers and professionals to become more vulnerable in our classrooms and workplaces. This, fundamentally, is the work of the first stage of the Movement

Model: the inner life of the individual. The work is not about changing others but transforming ourselves. Short circuit this work, and the other stages become unattainable.

My recovery led me to teach a humanities class at Valencia College called, "What's Love Got to Do With It?" I challenged students to explore the historical and philosophical meaning of love and how they might live a loving life, including service to humanity. While some colleagues ridiculed the class, I knew from my personal experience the possibilities for student transformation through a curriculum so seemingly counter-cultural.

SECOND STAGE: COMMUNITY OF MUTUAL ENCOURAGEMENT AND SUPPORT

The seeds for the Peace and Justice Initiative (PJI) at Valencia College were planted in that class and two other places on campus: a colleague's Peace Studies course and a faculty and staff renewal program, offered in connection with the Center for Formation in Higher Education (now The Center for Renewal and Wholeness in Higher Education, CRWHE), which focused on the alignment of soul and role.

The renewal program was based on a retreat model grounded in Parker's *The Courage to Teach*. Facilitators invited us to listen deeply to one another, pay attention to our own inner teachers, turn to wonder, and speak our truth—ground rules for encouraging meaningful dialogue and tools we could then use in our day-to-day work at the college. We also explored our birthright gifts, the light and shadow in our lives, and practiced habits of the heart that allowed us to grow as individuals and within community. In those circles of trust, we experienced safe space where we could ask open and honest questions, become vulnerable with one another, and learn how to be fully present to each other in moments of pain and triumph.

Elaine Sullivan, CRWHE facilitator, introduced us to the power of story. Sharing our life experiences brought heart into the room. We came to know each other more intimately and in a way that opened us to being challenged and changed by the life experiences of others. The transformation which took place went beyond the theoretical frameworks that define academic life.

The retreats were invitational and open to all; a core group emerged early on. That core group of individuals remains core, committed to one another personally and professionally. We became a community of practitioners who could face and endure conflict from within and without. An integrated and interdisciplinary group formed among us on campus. The power of story became a philosophical framework that informed the work of PJI.

Now the retreats attract up to 40 people from across the college with new people joining in each year. As more people participated in the retreats and gatherings on campus, communities of congruence formed. Many colleagues had been doing the work of peace and justice quietly and behind closed doors. As they discovered others in step with them, isolation decreased. Faculty members literally began to open their office doors, and employees leading social justice clubs were especially drawn to the movement. Knowing there were like-minded people on campus working toward the same end encouraged us to go forward. Together we posed the big questions: *What would a culture of peace look like at Valencia? A culture of justice? A culture of Peace and Justice?*

The core group of practitioners hosted World Café

conversations on the campuses to explore these questions. A clear need emerged for healthier ways to handle conflict, so we launched efforts to transcend the paradigm of conflict on our campus. The Peace and Justice Initiative, through one-on-one conversations and in retreat settings, drafted our mission and adopted Principles for How to Treat Each Other, modeled after the CRWHE Touchstones with input from Peter Block's work on community building. These principles became a common language and shared practices among the core group of practitioners.

Realizing the work began with the roots, we embarked on an intentional time of focusing on our values with faculty and staff. The Initiative sought consultation and training from experts in the fields of wholeness and renewal, nonviolence, conflict transformation, and peace studies. But we were careful to expand our scope gradually, to grow our movement organically. Our ultimate goal was to impact the culture of the college. We frequently reminded ourselves, "This is a 10-year project!"

As our work expanded over several years, the group grew and the Principles spread across campus; the decision was made to integrate them into everything we did. We read them at the beginning of meetings, events and workshops. One colleague had her students write about them in her speech class; other faculty followed. Soon the Principles were being used everywhere on campus: in our first-year experience course for students, by Human Resources during the on-boarding process for new employees, in the tenure process for new faculty, and in workshops, academic divisional meetings, and student-led organizations.

During this formative time, we also gathered to discuss values,

PRINCIPLES FOR HOW WE TREAT EACH OTHER
Our Practice of Respect and Community Building

1. **Create a hospitable and accountable community.** We all arrive in isolation and need the generosity of friendly welcomes. Bring all of yourself to the work in this community. Welcome others to this place and this work, and presume that you are welcomed as well. Hospitality is the essence of restoring community.

2. **Listen deeply.** Listen intently to what is said; listen to the feelings beneath the words. Strive to achieve a balance between listening and reflecting, speaking and acting.

3. **Create an advice free zone.** Replace advice with curiosity as we work together for peace and justice. Each of us is here to discover our own truths. We are not here to set someone else straight, to "fix" what we perceive as broken in another member of the group.

4. **Practice asking honest and open questions.** A great question is ambiguous, personal and provokes anxiety.

5. **Give space for unpopular answers.** Answer questions honestly even if the answer seems unpopular. Be present to listen not debate, correct or interpret.

6. **Respect silence.** Silence is a rare gift in our busy world. After someone has spoken, take time to reflect without immediately filling the space with words. This applies to the speaker, as well – be comfortable leaving your words to resound in the silence, without refining or elaborating on what you have said.

7. **Suspend judgment.** Set aside your judgments. By creating a space between judgments and reactions, we can listen to the other, and to ourselves, more fully.

8. **Identify assumptions.** Our assumptions are usually invisible to us, yet they undergird our worldview. By identifying our assumptions, we can then set them aside and open our viewpoints to greater possibilities.

9. **Speak your truth.** You are invited to say what is in your heart, trusting that your voice will be heard and your contribution respected. Own your truth by remembering to speak only for yourself. Using the first person "I" rather than "you" or "everyone" clearly communicates the personal nature of your expression.

10. **When things get difficult, turn to wonder.** If you find yourself disagreeing with another, becoming judgmental, or shutting down in defense, try turning to wonder: "I wonder what brought her to this place?" "I wonder what my reaction teaches me?" "I wonder what he's feeling right now?"

11. **Practice slowing down.** Simply the speed of modern life can cause violent damage to the soul. By intentionally practicing slowing down we strengthen our ability to extend non-violence to others—and to ourselves.

12. **All voices have value.** Hold these moments when a person speaks as precious because these are the moments when a person is willing to stand for something, trust the group and offer something he or she sees as valuable.

13. **Maintain confidentiality.** Create a safe space by respecting the confidential nature and content of discussions held in the group. Allow what is said in the group to remain there.

Prepared by the Peace and Justice Institute with considerable help from the works of Peter Block, Parker Palmer, the Dialogue Group and the Center for Renewal and Wholeness in Higher Education

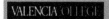 valenciacollege.edu/pjl   peaceandjustice@valenciacollege.edu   PEACE AND
407-582-2291   JUSTICE INSTITUTE

visions and purpose, guided by two of Parker's books, *A Hidden Wholeness: The Journey toward an Undivided Life* and *Healing the Heart of Democracy: The Courage to Create a Politics Worthy of the Human Spirit*. When I worried that our work might be futile, a waste of boundless energy, we would come together for another book study or retreat and my fears were quieted. Energized and renewed by the steadfast commitment to our shared passion and work, I woke one night with the words, *All People. All Voices. All Matter.* The vision was there: solid, real.

The image of a tree became the metaphor: branches were our communities of congruence; the trunk symbolized the soul of

Conflict Resolution
Service   Nonviolent Communication
Mind, Body, Spirit   Interfaith Understanding
Environment   Social Justice
Community
Global Awareness   Peace
Heart Soul
Values

each individual and the soul of the work for peace and justice; the roots grounded us in the values undergirding our initiative.

In this second stage, Parker, standing on the shoulders of Margaret Mead, counsels it's important to resist those who cannot imagine that a small group of people can change the world. He adds nay-sayers can be respectfully acknowledged, yet not empowered.

Following his advice, we chose to live in a conversation of "possibilities," one Peter Block outlines as essential to building community. Our core group became the Possibilities Group; the overarching work was the Peace and Justice Initiative. When we encountered people from across campus, including the library or student affairs, etc., who resonated with the work, we invited them to be a part of the Possibilities Group.

Today we have Possibilities Groups which are the grass roots leadership of PJI on all campuses and in different sectors, including legal and judicial, first responders, and education. Through this model we have planted seeds and deepened our roots, becoming a powerful force for the movement that ultimately shifted the culture of the college toward a peace and justice consciousness.

We have even compared ourselves to the movement at West Virginia University in the 1970's when they began a women's studies program. Like them, we have been laughed at and discouraged in many ways. And like them, we have formed an advisory council of strong and influential citizens that would support our work and could speak up for its benefits, if and when the college might try to shut down the program. These advocates outside the Valencia organization signal that this movement has implications for our community beyond the college walls.

THIRD STAGE: GOING PUBLIC

PJI first went public in 2011 by holding a retreat open to all Valencia employees and hosting a scholar-in-residence with workshops open to the entire Valencia community. Elaine

Sullivan masterfully introduced participants to the inner work needed to build trusting relationships and do the hard work of peace and justice. The retreats, facilitated by Elaine since 2002, attracted a growing number of participants as the years progressed.

We printed the Principles on cards, published lesson plans on how to use them, and invited all faculty to introduce them into their classrooms. We eventually printed poster size versions and offered them to faculty and staff to hang in offices and classrooms. We started a newsletter to tell the story of our work and invited students to join in. We hosted our annual Global Peace Week and Conversations on Justice events and developed a peace and justice studies curriculum.

As we went public, the issue of race emerged on our campus. Faculty of color with whom we'd built trusting relationships privately expressed concerns about racism in the academic institution. These conversations pre-dated the national attention to our area created by the killing of Trayvon Martin in the neighboring town of Sanford, Florida, placing PJI in a place to bring this issue to the attention of college leaders.

We invited Dr. Peggy McIntosh, an international leader on white privilege and equity work, to the campus. Additionally, we sent colleagues, including myself, to the Seeking Educational Equity and Diversity (SEED) Project in California (founded by McIntosh) for training in creating equitable and inclusive classrooms. After that training, PJI facilitators led SEED seminars which explored systems of privilege and oppression through "a balance of the scholarship of the self and the scholarship on the shelf," an idea coined by Emily Style, another SEED founder.

As we developed our skills to explore difficult conversations about not only race and privilege but also homophobia, classism and sexism, our country exploded with the killings of Michael Brown, Eric Gardner, Sandra Bland and so many more.

Bringing together all we'd learned through inner work in our retreats, ways of transforming conflict, and SEED training, we responded with Conversations on Race. Now public, we were prepared to help people explore a subject Now the retreats attract up to 40 people from across the college with new people joining in each year—.race—that most Americans feared and avoided.

The City of Orlando took note and, in 2015, invited us to lead a Conversation on Race at the Mayor's annual Neighborhood and Community Summit. Community leaders wanted this workshop to be introduced in all city districts, an idea first resisted by city officials. However, when incidences of excessive use of force and a call for the resignation of the Chief of Police came, we were called in to lead the crisis response. An outgrowth was Orlando Speaks, dialogues between citizens and police meant to build relationships and mutual understanding.

PJI was called in again when employees became targets of racial slurs. The city contracted with us to lead workshops for 3,000 employees, including police and fire fighters. *Conversations in Inclusiveness* integrated our Principles with an exploration of our multicultural selves, early messages and implicit bias. Non-profit and community groups asked us to offer these same workshops; within one academic year, more than 25,000 people were introduced to the Principles for How We Treat Each Other.

We made the transition from "Initiative" to "Institute" in

2015 when our focus broadened from campus to community and we considered the possibilities for impact in the greater central Florida region. As we secured contracts with the City of Orlando and other organizations, now we had a source of revenue for the foundation of a sustainable PJI program.

During this stage of "going public," PJI developed these Commitments as a framework for our program:

Commitments of a Peace and Justice Practitioner

Regarding every citizen as a rising peace and justice practitioner, the commitments of a practitioner are as follows:

- **Places relationship as central to the work, focusing on the culture of collaboration.**

- **Encourages a reflective practice to support self-awareness, meaning and purpose, using mindfulness practices and emotional intelligence.**

- **Addresses conflict as a source and opportunity for growth and transformation.**

- **Uses the tools of story, dialogue and peaceful communication while practicing the Principles for How We Treat Each Other in order to create meaning.**

- **Supports a community of inclusive excellence in which all voices are heard and valued.**

- **Engages in the exploration of the "other" with an acknowledgement of our inherent interdependence.**

- **Recognizes that there can be no peace without justice for all.**

FOURTH STAGE: TRANSFORMING THE SYSTEM OF PUNISHMENT AND REWARD

Early on, we told ourselves, peace and justice on the Valencia campus is a 10-year project. Now in our 11th year, we are entering the fourth phase: transforming the system and reaping alternative rewards.

Perhaps one of the greatest rewards for me personally is working with a community of practitioners dedicated to a common vision. To be connected on an intellectual and emotional level, to share a common passion for building the culture of peace and social justice, has added meaning and purpose to my personal and professional life.

An additional reward comes from knowing that the movement has changed the culture of the college. I've seen the hearts of many naysayers gradually change. Some have actually joined us. I've seen colleagues emerge from behind closed doors, witnessed careers revitalized, helped newcomers to our campus find ways to add their gifts to the movement underway.

PJI makes room for everyone. The result is a broad-based, inclusive movement that gives voice to those who sometimes struggle to find a voice and to those who felt lost or overlooked within the institution. The PJI Movement, which grew largely outside the organizational structure and boundaries of the college, now impacts the entire institution. This is the paradox inherent in the Movement Model's fourth stage.

Five years after PJI came into formal existence, Dr. Sandy Shugart, our college president, told me, "You have changed the conversation at the college. And changing the conversation is the necessary step to changing the culture." After our work with the City of Orlando, he named PJI one of the college's strengths. Had we needed that affirmation and positive feedback in the beginning, we would never have persevered.

In explaining his Movement Model, Parker Palmer writes: "We sometimes get perverse satisfaction from insisting that organizations offer the only path to change. Then, when the path is blocked, we can indulge the luxury of resentment rather than seek an alternative avenue of reform and we can blame it all on external forces rather than take responsibility upon ourselves."

I'm grateful for those of us who decided to live divided no more and sought an alternative avenue at Valencia College. Through PJI, we have established a common language and common practices that help us model a new way of being in the world, a new way of interacting with and teaching students in the classroom, a way of leading that invites honesty, authenticity, openness and integrity.

We know the power of our reward from the inside out: community, connection, and witnessing a group of committed people change the world where we work and live.

Rachel Allen is a life-long educator and practitioner who supports others to practice and educate for peace and justice in their work and personal lives. At Valencia College in Orlando, Florida, Rachel is a tenured Professor of Humanities and founding member and director of the Peace and Justice Institute. Rachel is a proud parent of two young children; they live in Maitland, Florida. Rachel can be reached at Rallen39@valenciacollege.edu

Wholeness is a Way of Being and not a Destination

By Fred Amador

Growing up I never really needed a lot of outside stimulation.

I had a vibrant inner life, and I would spend a lot of time by myself, journaling, reflecting and thinking about things. I always felt weird that I was not interested in most of the things my friends found so fascinating. I actually enjoyed being alone.

I started my journey toward wholeness in 2001 when I first participated in CRWHE facilitator training in Taos, New Mexico. I remember discovering so many different ways to explore parts of myself that I had kept hidden in small dark compartments. I really got in touch with my creativity and allowed myself to play a lot more in life.

That year was my second as a counseling faculty member at Phoenix College, and I was still learning about my job and my place in the circle. I was focused on my career advancement while neglecting most other aspects of my life. My whole identity was wrapped up in my career. My health suffered; I did not feel well most of the time.

When I participated in the CRWHE reflection and renewal circles, I tended to go with the flow. My best work friend always seemed to have a pulse on what readings or activities captured where we were as a group. During this time, I felt I was growing and exploring; I felt more whole.

In 2007 I was the focus person in a Clearness Committee for the first time. It was a life-changing experience. I became aware that as I climbed the ladder professionally I neglected my health, romantic relationships and having true joy in my life. As the focus person, I also explored the kind of life I wanted to create.

I shifted my focus in March 2008. I created a possibility of being healthy in my life. I started to notice that I focused on how I appeared to other people. I started working out, lost a lot of weight, and I gained self-confidence. I was also part of an educational program where I spent hours developing my leadership skills. My physical vitality was at an all-time high. I loved all the people I was inspiring with all the changes that I was making in my life. I traveled to New York and Boston. I felt whole and that I was attending to all aspects of my life.

The truth is that I neglected connecting with my family, people at work, and my mentees. My yard was full of weeds, and I did not keep up maintenance on my car. While I looked like I was whole on the outside, I felt fragmented on the inside and my environment reflected it.

I got married in April 2011. I became a stepdad to two children. I am not sure how my wife and I successfully made it through our first year of marriage. Less than three months after we were married I had an operation to remove thyroid cancer. Being a husband, stepfather, friend and family member was way more challenging than I thought it was going to be. It seemed like all I could do was disappoint everyone in my life. I felt completely broken. I felt like I was in the middle of the storm being blown around by every intense situation I faced.

Through reflection, community groups, mentors, counseling and self-reflection, I was able to heal and grow. I stopped blaming myself for everything and I started to feel more whole and complete. I have remained cancer free. I am a better husband, father and counselor.

The places I felt broken became whole; I felt stronger than ever before. I have realized that to be whole, to live divided no more, is not a destination; there is no finish line. Being whole and divided no more is a declaration and way of being.

I do not have to be perfect or have everything going well in my life to be whole and undivided. The imperfection is part of the wholeness.

The imperfection is a seed and an opportunity to grow, not a problem or reason to not accept all of who I am. When I forget this, I hide and divide myself into parts that I like about myself and things I dislike. I do not nor will I ever experience wholeness all the time. The opportunity comes when I see that I am not experiencing myself as a whole, and I can reflect on what I am doing.

The keys to wholeness for me are self-reflection and awareness. The essential practices are honesty, forgiveness, and grace.

Fred Amador is a counseling faculty member at Phoenix College for the last 18 years. He is very passionate about serving others and seeing them succeed! When he is not serving others he enjoys personal development and writing. He is known for his pop locking and robotic dancing when you least expect it. A native of Arizona, Fred can be contacted through email: fred.amador3@gmail.com

Pause

By Pam Davenport

Presume & extend welcome.
Be 100% present.
Listen deeply.
It is never "share or die."
No fixing.
Suspend judgment.
Maintain Confidentiality.
Identify assumptions.
Speak your truth.
Respect silence.
When things get difficult, turn to wonder.
Practice slowing down.

---CRWHE Touchstones: Practices that Create Safe Space

I am living The Touchstones.

Trying to do so has become a significant part of life for me, but I hesitate to make this bold statement. I can be quick to judge others or revert to my familiar hurrying, harried mode of operation. Still, I am trying, and every day these powerful ideas become more integrated into my way of being and interacting with my world. The Touchstones that we use in our Reflection, Renewal, and Role circles are boundary markers, for sure, yet they can also be foundations for living fully and mindfully and having a positive influence on others.

I suppose the following anecdote may be an excuse for writing about my grandson, but I hope the moment I describe illustrates the power inherent in simple precepts developed from Parker

Palmer's teachings and passed on to me many years ago by Elaine Sullivan, Sue Jones, and others from Richland College and the Center for Renewal and Wholeness in Higher Education (CRWHE). This power, this "force" as Obi-wan would say, is strong in circles of educators, leaders, and colleagues, as perhaps it is with a grandmother and a sixteen-month-old little boy.

We start with a piece of toast, a slice of Dave's Killer Organic Sprouted Wheat Bread, slathered in butter, and placed on the high chair tray by my son-in-law before he leaves for work. Baby Brackton and I sit quietly for a moment, look into each other's eyes, our expressions serious, and then he slowly lowers his head in the direction of the sacred food. He appears to be offering respect to the toast. Bowing once, he stops, and then I join him in offering our love and gratitude for this gift from the universe that provides for us: wheat, sun, water, yeast, salt, and so much more. We may bow two, three, even four times before Brackton gently touches the crust and pats the oily surface. We do not rush. Finally, we exchange looks again, and this time we smile in acknowledgement of all that is good. He takes his first bite.

Here is what I think: Brackton and I are celebrating our lives, our luck, our love, the fact that this boy and I live right here right now, that we are alive in this moment on this day, that we are together. The toast is crunchy and soft, warm with fat. We make a space and time for this ritual. When at last he finishes eating, I lift him from his chair and might be rewarded with a greasy face burrowed into my neck. I let him down and he waddles off to throw a grapefruit around the kitchen and race trucks across the floor. We won't even think about toast until we rise the next morning, and I sit before him, return his gaze, honor the space we share and the quiet of the moment.

Every day I try to remember to offer gratitude for reaching the age I am, for living to experience all the gifts that have come my way. Had I not become involved in wholeness and renewal work, I suppose I would spend sacred moments such as I described with my grandson, but I am not sure I would recognize their significance as I do now.

MY ONE REGRET

I sometimes hear myself say to others, *I regret only one thing, that I hurried my children when they were little.* In truth, I hurried everyone, especially myself.

As a young teacher I sometimes rushed my students through material to make sure we "covered" all we were supposed to. I am happy to say that long before I retired I came to my senses about the "coverage" issue, about how less is often more. I have lived long enough to recognize the importance of slowing down, of being 100% present. Surely I had heard such words before I started living with The Touchstones, but I didn't internalize them until I sat in circles, so many circles, with all kinds of people, and made these ideas a centerpiece of my life. If I had not sat quietly with Brackton, I might not have noticed that this baby boy was involving me in a moment of reflection and gratitude as forceful as any in a place of worship.

Sometimes the moment, the pause, can take years, can take that long for me to gain perspective, to escape my judgmental head. One day, trying to write a poem, I decide to revisit a distant memory and try to find why I hold onto an image of an injured deer and a friend; a foggy recollection of a misty day when nothing of particular note happened, except for the fawn on the mountain road. In my memory, the car I am driving emerges from a furious downpour, and suddenly before us is a baby deer on the wet pavement. Seeing her takes my breath away. It is a freeway, no chance of helping this poor animal, and I find the whole thing unbearable. Like many, I am particularly sensitive to animals in pain or danger, to how terrified they must be when they have no frame of reference for the experience as it happens. The friend with me does not appear to be affected as I am by the fawn's predicament, and for some reason I feel it is a failing on her part. Yet that day years later, as I try to write a poem that never comes to fruition, in the space created by that attempt to write, in that pause, I recognize that my friend is the fawn in my memory, that she is suffering herself. I finally turn to wonder and feel a rush of love for both the animal and my friend.

I also remember a day when 30 employees from my college met at the C.O.D. Ranch in Oracle, Arizona, for the first of many Reflection, Renewal, and Role Retreats. Before my facilitation partner and wonderful friend Darby Heath and I start leading these retreats, Elaine and Sue are facilitating this inaugural one. People from all employee groups gather in a barn, and all is going smoothly for us, The Touchstones very much abiding in the space. That is, until someone interrupts our facilitators and voices her concerns that not everyone present knows who Parker Palmer is, that they might not understand what is being discussed.

I sit stunned.

I figure this person must be referring to non-faculty, maybe particularly the maintenance staff members who are present. I have faith in Elaine and Sue and in these participants that they will indeed understand the third things, the stories and poems so gracefully shared, that the circle will hold them gently, will afford all of us that safety and regard. Later that first day, one of the janitors speaks up in the circle; she tells us of how she loves to clean the college gym before a basketball game, how she imagines the players and spectators appreciating the clean and comfortable environment for the competition and celebration. I love her story; we all do, and I feel so grateful for The Touchstones that prevented my own hotheaded propensity to address the faulty logic in the earlier comment, feel grateful for listening, for honoring the space between judgment and reacting, for turning to wonder. My colleague has a well-deserved reputation for protecting others; she cares about everyone's welfare. Granted, she is excellent at "fixing," and sometimes this is what students and employees need; she means well. Yet our circle does not need fixing: we take a collective pause, the moment passes, and The Touchstones are respected.

DOUBLE CONFIDENTIALITY

A few days ago I was at an annual writing retreat that has been going for 18 years. This event is an informal gathering of friends. We simply write together in response to prompts; through the stories and sharing, we discover our personal truths and have grown to love one another deeply. Yet I have carried with me for a year a concern about our group, a fear that questions posed in the circle about the stories shared at our readings might inhibit our writing. Before we begin, I tell the group about double confidentiality and ask if they are willing to invoke this practice for our retreats. All agree, and one woman says, "I've actually been thinking that we should begin each retreat with The Touchstones." She has been at many of our college and district events where we begin with the ritual of reading The Touchstones and it turns out has carried them with her for many years.

I have no idea how many times I have run into people who were with us for Reflection, Renewal, and Role and say they try to live according to The Touchstones. Sometimes they will pull a wrinkled list out of their wallets. Zen master Thich Nhat Hanh, global spiritual leader and peace activist, says we can make the world a better, more peaceful place by the way we interact with whomever we encounter. He helps me calm down when I feel responsible for the people who are suffering, when I feel guilty because I'm not on the streets protesting all the injustices causing others harm.

My way is to recognize how often what is needed is a pause. My way is to live by The Touchstones.

There are so many reasons to pause. I will let Buddhist teacher Pema Chodron have the last word, at least for the moment:

When we pause, allow a gap and breathe deeply, we can experience instant refreshment. Suddenly, we slow down, look out, and there's the world.

Pam Davenport spends most of the year in the Arizona desert where she draws on the seemingly stark landscape for inspiration for writing poetry. The best years of her decades in higher education were those spent leading retreats and campus gatherings for Reflection, Renewal, and Role. She is grateful for the rewarding experiences and enduring friendships. You can reach her by email at pam.davenport4@gmail.com

Horse Sense

By Katie O'Brien

"I think I'm the horse," I admitted to my husband, Bill.

This realization dawned on me a week after we had hosted the initial session of what we, at Rio Hondo College, call Reflection & Renewal (R & R) experiences. At that time, I had worked as a community college counselor and instructor for the Extended Opportunity Programs and Services (EOPS) for high risk, low-income students for nearly 15 years, and my husband was an independent educational consultant. The previous Thursday, we'd volunteered our time and our home to hold the first of a monthly discussion series on Parker Palmer's book, *The Courage to Teach*.

To a sane observer, all seemed to have gone well. We'd hosted an engaged cross-section of faculty and enjoyed some heartfelt discussion and reflection. That's why Bill was so puzzled at how agitated I was later that day when all I could focus on were the imperfections. This person tending to dominate, that person too quiet; me, awkwardly attempting to explain the work of formation, which has to be experienced to be known. I was tied up in a knot of anxiety before, during, and after the gathering and was now bereft at how inept I felt.

A few days later, Bill and I tuned into a documentary on equestrian competition. One Olympian, when asked about the key to her success, stated succinctly, "I have to remember that I'm not the horse." In a hand-slap-to-the-forehead moment, it struck me that the problem with our first R & R experience had little to do with my own inadequacies or how my colleagues did or didn't meet my expectations. The problem was that I was acting like I was the horse.

Formation work is about opening up a space for the soul to emerge so that those gathered can listen for their own inner wisdom, to enable a reconnection to one's purpose and gifts. The ego machinations I was racing through were certainly beside the point. True, a skilled facilitator like a skilled rider may be instrumental in the process, but only in as much as she enables the work, as a rider does the horse, to flourish.

The book group was our inaugural effort after Bill and I had both been prepared as facilitators by the Center for Renewal and Wholeness in Higher Education (CRWHE). I'd love to report that this early realization freed me from such misguided pre-occupations as we continued to offer these experiences.

I'd be lying.

I remember preparing for one of our first overnight weekend retreats taking place in Lake Arrowhead in the San Gabriel Mountains about two hours from the campus. Bringing together music, poetry and film to prompt inner work joyfully engaged me; however, thoughts of actually facilitating the retreat untethered my performance anxiety. That anxiety ratcheted up to a fever pitch when I received a retreat application from a colleague with whom I had locked horns in the past and now judged to be purposefully divisive. I thought, *Yes, all on campus are welcome, but him?*

I jumped to the assumption that his coming was a dark move to derail me and the formation work I so valued. Certain his presence would poison the weekend, I crafted an ever-so-clever email trying to explain formation in such a way that he would decide he had better things to do with his weekend. Fortunately, some impulse of greater light nudged me to copy my husband. Bill immediately responded, "Your slip is showing!"

What slip? I'm merely offering this person a fuller picture of Reflection and Renewal! But Bill exposed a set of blinders I couldn't ignore. I retrieved the email before this colleague could read it. I clearly was in need of a great deal of reflection and self-examination myself! In the days leading up to the retreat, I did a lot of journaling and praying and talked about the situation with my therapist. She offered me a necessary reframe: "Katie, do you really think he would give up his entire weekend simply to irritate you?"

As a group of approximately 20 staff and faculty, including this colleague, gathered around a fire Saturday evening to share tales and laughter after a day of intensive sessions, I exhaled. With Bill's support as co-facilitator and the grace that flows when soulful spaces are co-created, I saw this man sought what we all did—a weekend of heartfelt exploration and connection. While he and I never became best buddies, we caught each other's eyes as we left on that final morning, tacitly laying down the worst assumptions about each other, acknowledging a new appreciation that our differences sprung from equally valid wells. I still wince at the recollection of how my "it's all about me" shadow threatened to trample the essential spirit of the work.

REINING IN MY SHADOW

Whether this shadow emerged as a result of being the caboose in a five-kid train and/or a deep seeded push-pull relationship with the spotlight, I'm not certain. But it took me several years of retreat preparation and facilitation to come to understand that I am not the horse; to more gracefully walk what often felt like a very fine line; to bring my authentic gifts to the work while reining in the performance preoccupation that threatens to knock the experience off-stride.

Acknowledging this tendency poses a challenge in "going public." I've usually felt quite comfortable allowing my authenticity to roam free; I think that is why I have felt so at home in formation work.

When I sat in my first formation circle in Steamboat Springs in the summer of 2002, and we used poetry and music and journaling to reflect on our "true selves," I looked around thinking, "So this is a thing? Wow!" I felt as if I had unknowingly clicked my heels together, and like Dorothy, found "there's no place like home." While I wasn't even aware I'd been in search mode, it was likely no coincidence that my husband and I had been gifted with Parker Palmer's *Let Your Life Speak* mere months before this pre-conference retreat. After being prepared as a facilitator the following year, I was so certain of the value of formation that I convinced my husband to also attend the training one week before his doctoral dissertation defense!

I felt so comfortable in this realm, my ongoing challenge wasn't so much *if* I should go public, but *how* to do so in a way that was in service to the work, to the movement model Parker described, and not my ego. When I moved into the role of Staff Development coordinator on campus shortly after our initial book group, I had an additional venue in which to explore this challenge.

One of my responsibilities in my new role was to convene two pre-semester convocations, called FLEX days. I would kick off the mornings in our campus theater with announcements and an overview of the days that offered keynotes and breakout sessions for more than 400 faculty and staff. After a few semesters at the podium, I felt a tug of war between just getting on with the day as quickly as possible and, if inspiration presented itself, offering a story, quote, or invitation to reflect that seemed appropriate for that particular time and place.

Beneath my struggle was a seminal question: would I be seizing an opportunity to be "seen" in a venue not intended for such things? It was one thing to have folks voluntarily respond to a retreat invitation, but no one had elected me "Inspirer-in-Chief." And yet standing at the microphone looking at the faces of my colleagues, I longed to spark conversation about the purpose and heart that underlies our work as educators at our best.

TAKING THE PLUNGE

On a winter day in 2011, I took the plunge. I recounted a story and posed a question that I normally would have reserved for a retreat setting. I shared that 10 years prior, I'd traveled with my husband to New Zealand for consulting work at Auckland University of Technology (AUT). When we met with a small group to discuss expectations, a vice president informed us that AUT incorporated many Maori traditions into their way of doing business, including the welcoming of guests to the campus with a Maori Blessing, a "Song of Welcome" that represented who they were as a people. She went on to say that tradition called for guests to respond with their own song representing who they were and where they came from. She indicated this certainly wasn't required, but we were invited to do so.

My husband, not being quite as enthralled with center stage as I, said we'd be honored, but weren't prepared to sing. So the program began with the entire group standing and singing a moving Maori blessing. Bill graciously thanked them and began his remarks. He introduced me a bit later to talk about a student retention program we'd implemented at Rio Hondo. Inspired, I suggested we circle back to the song idea for a minute. It was a good thing Bill was sitting behind me so I couldn't see his reaction to my "bright idea."

"We've traveled from America," I said. "How about we sing a song that represents us, *This land is your land, this land is my land?*" Immediately several AUT folks proclaimed they knew the song and asked if we'd like some help. Together, we sang a verse and chorus of this Woody Guthrie classic.

Just two months earlier, we had witnessed the Twin Towers go down. To be welcomed in this manner and joined in a song that speaks to a sense of expansiveness and belonging at that moment in time was profoundly moving.

As I finished this tale, I nodded at the new Rio Hondo employees sitting in the first row, scanned the rest of the theater, and asked, "What song would represent us? What song would capture who we are and what we aspire to individually and as a community?"

While some may have checked out or been irritated by my digression, I began to hear from others folks, on the mornings of subsequent FLEX Days, "Katie, do you have a story for us?" For years after that, I continued to be transparent with faculty and staff about who I am and what's meaningful in my life and work.

But this way of being took longer to find its way into my classroom. As an instructor, I'm fiendish about protecting class time to ensure I "cover" all the material. This rigidity loosened one day in fall of 2016 in a College and Life Success class I was teaching. Rio Hondo is a Hispanic-Serving Institution (HIS), and that class was made up entirely of young Latina and Latino students who'd just graduated from high school. It was one week after the election of Donald Trump as President, and aware of some of the darker campaign rhetoric, I felt I needed to carve out time to help students process the election.

Without conscious intent, I brought to bear the tools I usually reserved for a retreat setting. I first asked the students to reflect individually on their reactions to the election and their hopes and fears for themselves, their families and friends; I then opened up the space for voluntary sharing. Adrian spoke of his fear for his aunt in Las Vegas who didn't have papers. Desiree heartbreakingly asked, "Why do they hate us?" Yessenia, her voice trembling, admitted, "The place I left was so dangerous, so desperate. I'm terrified of being sent back."

The students began to ask for my opinion. Luckily my ego was not holding the reins that day. I sensed how important it was to keep the space as open as possible, without any voice of supposed authority unintentionally shutting down a more hesitant contribution.

Then Ernesto raised his hand. He was a quiet, articulate young man who often kept his backpack on the entire class, cramming himself uncomfortably into his desk for nearly an hour and a half. On this day, he admitted how anxious he had been since the election. His two younger siblings were born here, but neither he nor or his parents resided here legally. Being ready to move with everything in his possession at a moment's notice might be the most comfortable position he could bear.

OFFERING MY TAKE

When the time seemed right, I offered my take. I began with my recognition of how **real** racism and prejudice is and my feeling that people voted as they did for many reasons, not all of which had to do with divisive rhetoric. I shared how many of us, even if white and middle-aged and privileged with citizenship, were also deeply upset, demoralized, and anxious for what this meant for our neighbors and for our country. In the end, I underlined the need to be cautious and self-protective, while also holding onto the light and aspirations that brought them to our campus.

Understanding a return to "content" at this point would be

foolhardy, an inspiration hit me. I pulled up a poem that I'd used before in R & R work, *It Is I Who Must Begin* by Vaclev Havel. I read it aloud and then invited students to read lines; different voices filled the room. When we came to the final line, I heard from Marco, a student who had never uttered a word in class: *"Whether or not all is lost, entirely depends upon whether or not I am lost."*

As students streamed out, a sense of sacredness hung in the air. Some had tears in their eyes. One asked for a hug. A few offered a quick nod. This scene reminded me of the atmosphere at the end of our R & R retreats —a sense of gratitude and relief that, in a dangerous world, safe spaces and experiences of shared humanity were still possible.

My students had reminded me of one of formation's most powerful lessons; that if I keep my ego out of the saddle, I am rewarded with a gift beyond measure, the honor of witnessing brave and vulnerable souls show themselves. What a gratifying ride it's been!

Author's Note: All student names have been changed.

Katie O'Brien has served Rio Hondo College as a counselor, instructor and professional development coordinator for 30 years and was named the 2018 Distinguished Faculty Member of the Year. She and her husband, Dr. Bill Grevatt, now a Jungian psychotherapist, live and travel from a home base in Whittier, California. She loves good writing, good food, good wine, good dogs, and the gentle whisper of rustling chimes. She can be reached via email at kobrien@riohondo.edu

Living Outside the Lines

By Jeff Hood

I came of age during the Cold War 50's and the awakening 60's. Seeking a path through what I perceived to be a civilization disastrously divorced from our source, our mother, our garden, I've done my little bit to get to know her blue/green essence. As with our dreams, I think she reveals herself through the soulful language of wonder, imagery, mystery and emotion. And since I "stop[ped] by woods on a snowy evening" with Robert Frost 60 years ago, I've been attempting to express those essential relationships through poetry, for it is a language that has the least restriction and most opportunity for painting outside the lines. Poetry is my forum for singing exuberance, wailing grief, and cringing in fear.

This first poem, *Good Friday*, dances with the personal and political. It describes a unique relationship formed through years of working (that is, hammer and nail, shovel and cement; sweaty, splintery, real work) with a man who would be put at risk were I to name him in print. We would never acknowledge the intimacy we've found. That would be entirely unnecessary and cross too many cultural taboos. Soulful connection need not always be voiced for it flows between us with a shared jalapeño at lunch, a nod at the work finished at the end of the day, an extra warm pair of gloves offered as snow begins to fall.

Good Friday

How do I reconcile my friend's refusal to file federal income taxes despite the fact that he's done it for the last fifteen years, because he might be identified and deported?

*I ran into him and his sister Good Friday noontime.
They'd just returned from a pilgrimage,
a six-hour walk to the Santuario de Chimayo,
something New Mexicans have been doing
for generations, before our borders
needed to be defended from aliens.*

*What could I say to this big-hearted man
whose smile illuminates his face,
whose palm when I grip it is strong and calloused
by years on a shovel, hammer, horse brush,
who came here with young children
to escape gangs and murder in his country,
to help them build a future in this strange land.*

*He once won $7,000 in a casino
and immediately bought a trailer
so his family could claim roots.*

*I hired him to help build my house one year.
Never a whisper that it was a palace in comparison to his.
He helped me butcher the pig to roast for our celebration,
but refused to attend, awkward of his language,
his work jeans, his culture,
not understanding he owned a seat at my table.*

*And how do I communicate any of this
to the people who would build a wall,
afraid of this gentle man with a light
shining out of his chest?*

A second poem crafted while spending a weekend at a friend's house in Dallas explores a different kind of soul pull, the one that comes through our wild world, or the little patches left of it. I've sought out some of the remotest places left on our planet, where footprints and trash are nonexistent. They are sacred cathedrals offering a union not available in cities. But we can't all go to those places without changing them forever. And fortunately, there are little chapels ringing with bird song and rushing water waiting behind the most ordinary backyards. They are not always comfortable. We find our refuse mixed with the rainbows, but our mother is there, calling us back to the simple passion we left in her garden.

Blue Gate

My friend's backyard
falls down progressively more wild
to a fence in which a blue gate opens.
A portal through which
a dark riot unkempt
calls me deep to where
water snake hunts fish
and raccoon hunts him.

They all fear me
no less than I fear myself,
Adam cast out,
forever looking back,
engaged in the contest
between tinkling rapid,
bird call, seed fall,
and erratic rush of auto over bridge.

Come with me now!
Red bird calls
from high in his tree
and I've seen his mate
sneak into the thicket.

The wilds have also taught me about going slow enough to pay attention to the important things. When I get away from my cell phone, my automobile, online banking, airplanes, texting, Facebook—all the busyness in which I too often lose my sense of self—I discover miracles moment to moment. Most rivers average four miles an hour; trying to push them faster belongs to those concerned with their profit margins and making appointments on time. Walking or floating at that pace we experience the eddies, comfortable little backwaters, time to breathe and collect ourselves; and we find the current, sometimes a riot and chaos of rapids, sometimes a rush and a whoop. Always an adventure in waking to Earth's blessings.

Life At Four Miles An Hour

I can walk four miles an hour
which is slower than my bicycle,
and notice the sunflowers blooming
with bees busy pollinating.

I can carry on a conversation
at four miles an hour,
and have time to go back to
a point brought up yesterday.

I can listen to you with no
fear for my own gain.

I can sort through my projections of you
to find who you are
at four miles an hour.

We travel four miles an hour
on the river,
and day after day we collect
the landscape

into ourselves
so that it supports us,

like the dried rose on my dashboard
reminding me of your love.

Faster is not better,
for I get ahead of my soul
and then who will notice
the sunflowers,
or take time to float the rivers,

or stop by the side of the road
to write this poem and weep.

One of the questions that has haunted and defined me ever since I played Biff in Death of a Salesman in High School is *"What's the point of going to work five days a week, driving through traffic, putting up with a boss, getting paid, coming home and doing it over again and again?"* Not to deny the simple joy of providing and house-holding, I've been looking for more as long as I can remember.

Are only the mystics allowed?

Are only the mystics allowed
to have mystical experiences?
Or is it something the rest of us can do?

On our hike today coming down the ridge
populated with pinon, an occasional pondo,
I don't remember if it was before or after
we stopped in awe of the view higher up
of snowfields reaching into the clouds,

that David spoke about Miranda's death
and her message to follow the light.
I glimpsed it, just a flash.
It could have been missed.
In a breath here and gone
beckoning, "It's simple, Jeff,
put out your hand."

Did Jesus do more?
It must have come and gone for him
like that, and he sorted through
all the expectations of others,
his fear of power, of his painful end,
doubt that he should have been a carpenter instead,
and found the courage to reach.

I hope these few lines have inspired you to go find a bit of earth that hasn't been tailored by human hands. The place may not be pretty, or even seem safe at first, but it is in those places that we find wonder, that our planet reveals herself to us in all her mystery, and there we uncover an essential part of ourselves, for we belong here, an integral part of her life.

Jeff Hood lives in Santa Fe, NM where he has an active practice of hiking, skiing and boating in the wonders of our Rocky Mountain West. He can be reached at jhood49x@gmail.com

A Journey into Connection and Wholeness

By Emily McRobbie

Everyone thinks of changing the world,
but no one thinks of changing himself.
---Leo Tolstoy

I often find solitude and freedom from the busyness of life while sitting mindfully on a special rock in the forest near my home. As I become aware of my breath, body and mind begin to relax and experience a sense of wonder and grace. I am able to sit with my inner landscape.

At first, I observe thoughts and with an open awareness, let them move through. A resistance to stillness follows, accompanied by passing emotions of frustration, sadness, anger and yearning. I sense the same emotions exist in others, including those who have hurt me, and gradually soften into compassion for our shared humanness. The present moment comes into better focus.

A deep calm emerges. This is a heart-connection with life, one nourished by yoga, mindfulness practices and formation work that I began more than 20 years ago.

AN INTRODUCTION TO FORMATION

Working as a Professional Development Coordinator at a community college led me to register for the 2003 *Teaching for a Change* Conference in Steamboat Springs, Colorado. There was an option to sign up for a pre-conference *Heart of the Teacher* retreat, and I entered into my first formation work without fully realizing what it would be. I suspect the other participants shared my uncertainty in those first hours.

In that two-day retreat, Dr. Sue Jones introduced a group of 20 diverse college educators to formation work. We joined in a circle to explore our inner landscapes and life journeys. There were moments of silence, opportunities to reflect and journal, and times to listen or share. Active listening and holding space were encouraged as we discovered our own answers. We became witnesses for one another.

THE DECISION TO LIVE UNDIVIDED

The opportunity to reflect on my work as an educator allowed me to explore the divided life I had been living. At the college, I was driven and always busy. In my home life, I craved silence, meditation and soul connection. At the time of the conference, I believed that professional and personal worlds needed to remain separate and distinct. Sitting in a circle with others who desired to find sacred space in their work as I did, I realized a longing for a life of deeper connection, one with a sense of wholeness. My journey with formation work began.

Before working at the community college and being introduced to formation, I worked as an elementary teacher and practiced yoga after work. The word yoga in Sanskrit translates to union or connection. The afternoon discipline helped me feel more grounded and present. I'd even taught some of my restless elementary students a few poses, and they loved them.

Like the formation experience, my first yoga teacher training was life-changing. I'd arranged a house swap on the Big Island, Hawaii, in 2005. Down the road was a retreat center named Kalani, which translates as "the heavens" in the Hawaiian language. Its mission was transformation via personal growth and healing. I wandered into this tropical setting and spotted a sign posted at the front desk advertising yoga teacher training to begin the following week. Impulsively, I signed up.

Two weeks of yoga and meditation practices lifted a veil. Each time I asked my teacher a question, she replied, "Go to the mat and the question will be answered." What often happened was that the questions transformed into a deeper awareness or dissolved altogether. Emotional trauma I'd carried since childhood energetically left my body and forgiveness naturally flowed. I felt healthier, lighter, freer and genuinely happy for perhaps the first time in years. I began to realize that these practices provided a way around the over-analytical mind and a backdoor into the unconscious where deeper healing and heart centering occur.

YOGA ON CAMPUS

After my training, I began offering yoga classes for employees and students at the college where I worked. Colleagues enjoyed the yoga lunch break and said they felt more relaxed moving into their afternoons. Students, when asked to reflect on their experience with yoga, shared stories of releasing addictions, improving their diets, reducing stress, discovering perseverance, and experiencing greater health and happiness.

Deeper connections began to form on campus. People who'd never taken a yoga class began to ask about it. The Human Resources department invited me to develop "Yoga for the Office" as an employee development workshop. I integrated personal exploration and health topics along with professional development sessions into our Employee Development Days.

After shifting into a new role of teacher education faculty at the same college, I was honored with the Faculty of the Year award. Simmering in the background all these years was a desire to engage again with formation work. I decided to use the award funds to attend the Renewal and Wholeness facilitator training in Taos, New Mexico, in 2012. Formation work was the catalyst for integrating my love for yoga in my work as an educator, and I was inspired to share formation with others.

MINDFULNESS INTEGRATION

A year after training as a formation facilitator, I received a lay-off notice from my faculty position. It came without warning; the college was eliminating its teacher education program. Faced with starting over, I began a daily meditation practice, something I'd been introduced to through yoga but had never engaged in on a regular basis. Morning meditation became an anchor.

After much soul-searching, I faced a decision about whether to return to school full-time and complete the doctorate I'd started years earlier. Before committing, I wanted to be certain I could continue to integrate my teacher self with my spiritual self, to be authentic. With some trepidation, I met with doctoral advisors at a nearby university to explain my interest in research about how mindfulness practices intersect with teaching and learning. The department chair replied, "Well, there's no one in the department conducting research in this area, but that's an interesting and timely topic."

Mindfulness is an umbrella term for practices grounded in present moment observation and involve the suspension of judgment or holding open curiosity about what is there without trying to change it. These practices, which are found in many cultures and traditions, can be taught in classes such as yoga, meditation, and tai-chi without philosophical or religious teachings.

Intrigued by the few programs introducing teachers to mindfulness practices, I reached out to the director of Passageworks, Dr. Rona Wilensky, who leads the SMART in

Education program. She welcomed my dissertation research and introduced me to an amazing community of educators.

Participants described how regular mindfulness practice supported personal transformation and holistic, human-centered educational environments. They reported how they became more patient, forgiving and resilient. They described how mindfulness enabled them to be calmer and more present with their students, and they experienced a strengthened capacity to better understand themselves and consider different perspectives. In essence, when a teacher engaged in mindfulness practices, they reported an improved relational quality with self and others.

NURTURING WHOLENESS IN EDUCATION

Mindfulness and formation work run counter to the behavioral and attitudinal norms of most educational institutions. Too often the demands, time limitations, and budget constraints that haunt educational systems tear at present-moment awareness and crowd intuitive spaces that might otherwise foster a more humane professional landscape. Yet when we attend to the whole person, whether teaching them a mindfulness practice or sitting in silence in a formation circle, teachers, students, and staff become more aware, forge deeper connections, and experience greater relational trust.

Mindfulness and formation work share much in common. Both are invitational, engage the whole person, and help people focus on being fully present. In formation work, we explore open-ended questions and suspend judgment individually and with each other.

- What does this poem prompt in me?
- Where am I right now in my life?

- What questions might I ask to help this colleague discover her own answer?

During a mindfulness practice, we suspend judgment in order to come into present moment awareness.

- How do I feel right now?
- What sensations or thoughts are present?
- Is this a pattern
- I have noticed?
- What changes the pattern?

During my two-decade journey with mindfulness practices and formation work, I have learned to listen more deeply, notice subtle conflict, and consider different ways to engage. As a college instructor in northern Arizona, I pay greater attention to my Native American students' struggle and try to use my position, as they move through a Western educational system, to help create a bridge for their success. I notice what a student or colleague is not saying during a meeting and ask more open-ended questions. I detect when I am out of balance more quickly and turn to a practice which helps center me. I am now less resistant to facing my imperfections. I move beyond the fear of vulnerability to more important aspects of work and life: finding connection and meaning with others.

Parker Palmer advocates inner reflection and connection with wholeness. In many of my classes, I share the following passage from his book, *The Courage to Teach,* with college students planning a career in education:

Teaching, like any truly human activity, emerges from one's inwardness, for better or worse. As I teach, I project the conditions of my soul onto my students, my subject, and our way of being together. The entanglements I experience in the classroom are often no more or less than the convolutions of my inner life. Viewed from this angle, teaching holds a mirror to my soul. If I am willing to look in that mirror and not run from what I see, I have a chance to gain self-knowledge—and knowing myself is as crucial to good teaching as knowing my students and my subject.

As educators, we can look into that mirror, not run from what we see, and provide safe spaces for colleagues and students to engage in the imperfect, unexpected, and generally messy process of knowing ourselves. This is a journey we can share, one of finding connection and nurturing wholeness.

Dr. Emily McRobbie recently accepted a new position as Assistant Professor of Adult & Higher Education at the University of Southern Maine. She and her husband, Eric Pepin, love to hike, travel, and spend time with good friends. She may be contacted through emilyjmcrobbie@gmail.com

Ginger Gray Squirrel
By RubyRenee Wood

Ginger gray squirrel,
I adore you!
In all of your twitchy, sniffy ways.

How dramatically you
Flick off hitchhiking fleas.
You alone have proven

How to stand your ground
With your steady gaze.
You taunt me with your

Licorice jelly bean eyes
And your fashion forward tail.
That tail!

Let your humble servant touch it!
No?!?
Does it feel prickly or soft?

Either way it is enchanting.
Next season
Everyone will wear one!

Oh my, your digging skills
So Exquisite!
I am honored to share

The secret of your nut stash.
Ginger gray squirrel,
I adore you!

RubyRenee Wood supports the arts as an Office Assistant to the Carlsen Center Performing Arts Series General Manager at Johnson County Community College. She lives in Kansas City, Missouri, where she pursues any and every type of creative expression with her darling husband CHVCK and cat Blanche. She can be contacted through e-mail: RubyRenee44@gmail.com

The Gift of Listening

By Karen Luke Jackson

At the 2001 meeting of the American Association of Community Colleges, I heard an answer to prayer. Sue Jones and Ann Faulkner introduced Parker Palmer's work and announced the opening of the Center for Formation in the Community College (CFCC, now the Center for Renewal and Wholeness in Higher Education, CRWHE).

Since the early 90's, Palmer's articles in *Weavings* and his books *The Promise of Paradox, To Know as We are Known, The Active Life,* and *In the Company of Strangers* had influenced me. I'd also attended an Institute for Servant Leadership where he'd led a three-day retreat focusing on topics like scarcity and abundance, identity and integrity, and rejoining soul and role. There I heard him describe a seasonal retreat series for K-12 teachers, a pilot project funded by the Fetzer Institute, in which educators were gathering in circles to remember "the who that teaches."

At the end of that conference, I approached Parker. "How can I get involved?" I asked.

At the time, I was working as Dean for Institutional Advancement at Blue Ridge Community College and completing my doctorate, a necessary step should I decide to seek a college presidency. For 10 years, I'd also been leading church retreats, hosting a women's spirituality group, and escaping to monasteries to nurture the inner life which fueled my outer work with students, faculty, staff, board members, and donors. Parker's approach of integrating education, community, and spirituality offered a way for these to come together for me, a path of integration and wholeness.

Gracious as always, Parker said, "The work we're doing now is for K-12 teachers, but there might be room for you. Let's stay in touch."

MOVING FROM SCARCITY TO ABUNDANCE

After that institute, I designed a county-wide planning project, incorporating some of Parker's principles of listening deeply and speaking one's truth. When more than 50 community leaders gathered to tackle a Welfare to Work Plan primarily targeted at single mothers, I invited them to vision from a place of abundance rather than scarcity. As a result, we developed a model for the state of North Carolina. People who'd watched me for years asked what had changed.

"I met this guy named Parker Palmer," I replied, "and I'm not sure where I'm headed."

My next encounter with Parker came two years later when I was granted leave at Blue Ridge to accept a one-year teaching position at Appalachian State University in Boone, North Carolina. My first day there, new faculty were given Parker's new book, *The Courage to Teach*. A professor who taught educational leadership had Parker quotes posted all over his office door. While teaching at App State, I traveled to nearby Warren Wilson College to hear Parker deliver an endowed lecture which later became the second chapter of a future book, *Let Your Life Speak*.

When my teaching year was over, I returned to the community college uncertain about my career path but aware that any work I pursued in the future had to take place at the intersection of education, community, and spirituality. The Center for Formation in the Community College (CFCC) seemed to offer just that!

FACILITATOR PREPARATION

In the summer of 2001, I attended the first CFCC facilitator preparation program. Community college faculty and staff from across the United States assembled in Taos, including people who'd had the benefit of Parker as a consultant on their campus for several years.

There I volunteered to be a focus person in a Clearness Committee. Five strangers held safe space for me to wrestle with whether or not to apply for community college presidencies. I walked out of that three-hour session unsure of my vocational path, but aware I needed to be engaged with folks who were committed to living an undivided life.

Stephen Mittelstet, president of Richland College in Dallas, Texas, served as one of my committee members. After returning to North Carolina, I wrote Steve to ask how Parker's work was unfolding on his campus. He invited me to do a post-doctoral fellowship, to "come and be another set of eyes." The next spring, I headed west to shadow Steve.

Among the learning outcomes we'd agreed upon was "to better understand how individual and group formation work affects organizational culture." When I arrived, I was amazed at Steve's instructions: "Sit in on any meetings, interview anyone on campus, attend the formation facilitator preparation program offered by Dallas County Community College District (DCCCD), go through our new employee orientation, and let me know what you need from me.

"And by the way, you're now an honorary Thunderduck!"

A Thunderduck? I thought. What's going on here?

I was quickly immersed in a culture that I later came to understand had prepared the soil for the seeds that Parker planted as he consulted with Richland and other colleges in the Dallas district. On a campus where a majority did not exist among the student population and more than 80 foreign languages were spoken, approximately 100 of the 400 employees had participated in or were currently engaged in formation activities. Some had attended introductory weekend retreats; others had participated in a year-long seasonal formation series.

These programs were offered through the college's professional development program, known on campus as the Thunderwater Organizational Learning Institute. Any faculty, administrator, or staff member could choose to participate, but no one was ever required to attend, honoring Parker's admonition that if an individual is mandated to do inner work, it will probably backfire.

BECOMING AN ANTHROPOLOGIST

I became an anthropologist, living among Thunderducks and yet not one of them. I attended President's Cabinet meetings, planning sessions for the upcoming accreditation renewal, employee orientation, DCCCD formation facilitator training led by Elaine Sullivan, and interviewed more than 20 individuals, including four vice presidents, the president and vice-president of the faculty association, the president of the professional staff association, college presidents from two sister institutions, and the director of the DCCCD Foundation.

I learned that The Touchstones, guidelines about how people were to "be with one another," had been integrated into daily campus interactions. For example, Steve opened his weekly leadership teams with silence and a check-in from each person sitting at the table. What was shared was not a performance report but the names of people at the college celebrating an accomplishment, facing illness, or grieving a loss, not unlike the opening check-in of a circle of trust. They then turned to the hard-hitting data analysis and quality enhancement which in 2005 garnered Richland the Malcolm Baldridge National Quality Award presented by the President of the United States, the first community college to receive that honor.

Steve told me that he often drew upon what he'd learned in formation circles as he made decisions. Since I'd been a fund-raiser, he shared this story: A few years after they'd been working with Parker, a donor offered Richland College a million-dollar gift. It came with strings attached. At the next Cabinet meeting, he asked his leadership team how the college might meet the stipulations. After bandying ideas about for about half an hour, Steve's stomach was churning. He stopped the conversation.

"I looked around and remembered half my leadership team had been in a circle of trust," Steve told me. "They knew about Clearness Committees, so I asked those folks to do nothing but ask me open, honest questions and the others to simply hold silence. At the end of that impromptu Clearness Committee, I knew why I had to refuse the money and what I needed to say to the donor. A gift with those conditions would divert us from our mission."

While conducting interviews, I intentionally sought out people who had not participated in formation work. Several expressed skepticism about the model and added they'd voiced their opinions freely, fearing no repercussions as they might have on another campus.

One Vice President, who hadn't found the time herself, volunteered that her secretary had been in a year-long retreat series and as a result seemed much happier in her work. "She even treats the students with more respect."

THE GIFT OF LISTENING

Toward the end of my time at Richland, I asked how Parker's work had influenced the vibrant, caring culture that had been nurtured at Richland for more than 20 years.

"We thought we knew how to listen," Steve answered, "but in truth, we were talking at and past each other. As a result, we encountered roadblocks and difficulties when we tried to implement decisions. Sometimes we even had to start over. Parker helped us learn how to truly listen to one another. Now, when another colleague is speaking, we hear what she says. Fewer headaches that way."

"Then by slowing down and getting clear on the front end," I teased, "you can move at speeds other institutions find dizzying."

As my time at Richland was coming to a close, I interviewed Cindy Johnson and Estrus Tucker and learned about the Center for Teacher Formation facilitator preparation program they had attended. Both lived in Fort Worth and were integrating Parker's circles of trust model in churches, nonprofit settings, and programs seeking racial justice.

I returned to North Carolina, jobless but with lots of contacts in K-12, community colleges, churches, and nonprofit settings. The question I held: *Where to from here?*

I knew I could not go it alone; community had been important all my life. I turned to John Fenner, a trusted colleague I'd work with for several years leading strategic planning and visioning processes. John had almost two decades of mediation and anti-racism work experience. The Center for Teacher Formation (now the Center for Courage & Renewal) was offering its first facilitator preparation for a cross-professional cohort. John applied and, as Parker writes, "way opened."

I've often said that Parker Palmer drew me into formation work and Elaine Sullivan taught me the finer points of creating safe-but-charged space for people to engage in inner work, of asking open and honest questions, and of confronting my own shadow. In April 2003, Elaine flew to western North Carolina to co-lead our first three-day offering. A late snow blanketed azaleas and dogwood blossoms as we drove into Montreat Conference Center for a retreat attended by more than 30 K-12 teachers, community college leaders, and nonprofit directors.

After that, John and I offered introductory programs and a seasonal retreat series for non-profit leaders, funded in part by the Z. Smith Reynolds Foundation and co-sponsored by the North Carolina Center for Nonprofits and Duke University's Nonprofit Leadership Program. I also worked with colleagues from the Center for Renewal and Wholeness in Higher Education and the Center for Courage & Renewal (CCR) to introduce Parker's Circle of Trust® at private and public universities, in clergy lay training, to small group ministries, and at interfaith gatherings.

When Duke University's Nonprofit Leadership Program announced an advanced program for seasoned nonprofit executives, I helped design the curriculum; Parker's work on identity and integrity became a foundational piece.

A group of Poor Clare Sisters in Greenville, South Carolina, discerning whether or not to build a new monastery, asked me to lead their process. I asked if they didn't need to find someone more familiar with their order.

"We think you're the right person," the abbess said, "because you've done all that Parker Palmer work!"

COURAGE OR FORMATION OR CIRCLES OF TRUST: IT WORKS

Whether Parker's model, which grows out of his Quaker roots, is referred to as *formation*, language drawn from the monastic model, or *circles of trust*, a phrase used to describe gatherings of two or more people engaged in deep listening, or *courage work*, a short-hand many CRWHE and CCR facilitators use, the wisdom it embodies cannot be limited to a retreat setting. When people listen to their Inner Voice, Inner Teacher, or True Self, they are changed and find it difficult to go back to their old ways. I've seen them integrate The Touchstones and reflective practices in work and family life. One woman used The Touchstones to hold more meaningful conversations with adults with disabilities served by her nonprofit organization. A Presbyterian minister introduced them to teens on a mission trip. I began to use open, honest questions with my children rather than give them advice.

As John O'Donohue writes in *The Question That Holds the Lantern*, "Once you start to awaken, no one can ever claim you again for the old patterns. Now you realize how precious your time here is. You are no longer willing to squander your essence on undertakings that do not nourish your true self.... Now you are...willing to put yourself in the way of change. You want your work to become an expression of your gift."

This 25-year journey has held many blessings. Two of the greatest are my relationships with Elaine Sullivan and John Fenner. Elaine has been a faithful companion and mentor, as I led retreats, wrote grants, and dealt with personal loss. John has been my co-creator, a sounding board, steady presence, and when needed, the voice of reason. And I've been fortunate to be associated with both Centers whose facilitators have tilled the soil and spread the seeds of Parker's work in the United States and abroad.

I give thanks for the gift of listening to that long-ago answer to prayer and for the opportunities which unfolded along the way. Each one-on-one encounter, each detour down a different path, and each circle I've been privileged to sit in, sometimes as a facilitator and sometimes as a participant, has helped me uncover my hidden wholeness. And I still have a long way to go.

Dr. Karen Luke Jackson convenes circles and companions people in the midst of major life transitions. She lives in a cottage on a goat pasture in Flat Rock, North Carolina, where she writes poetry, spins stories, and delights in the artistic pursuits of her three grandchildren, Jackson, Kaia, and Auden. You can reach her at kljluke@gmail.com

A Culture of Wholeness:
Of Thunderducks and Spirit of Place

With Steve Mittelstet

We are honored to share here some of the reflections of Dr. Stephen K. Mittelstet, President Emeritus of Richland College of the Dallas County Community College District (DCCCD) and Distinguished National Advocate, Center for Renewal and Wholeness in Higher Education. Mittelstet's support is an important part of the story of the partnership that resulted in the Center for Renewal and Wholeness in Higher Education (CRWHE), hosted by Richland College since 2008. You will find more about CRWHE in the final section of this book, as well as in some of the stories, but now, we want you to meet Steve.

Steve, what is a Thunderduck anyway?

R. Möbius Thunderduck (a.k.a. "Moby Duck") is the official Richland College mascot. All current and former students and

employees of Richland College are Thunderducks.

The responses to this oft-asked question, whether on campus or off, have many stories behind and under and through them, as does the life of Richland College (RLC) and its "Spirit of Place." Some have been passed down orally and others are now engraved on cmapus plaques. They are intricately woven together, as are the powerful stories in my personal life, beginning with bedtime stories my Oklahoma pioneer Grandma Eva told me when I was a toddler and throughout my nearly four-decade career at Richland College and now in my retirement.

I think the original story behind the Thunderduck name is pretty cool. According to Wrestling Coach Bill Neal, Thunderduck was RLC's state championship wrestling team's nickname for one of their beefy star teammates, whose walk was the source of his first nickname "Duck"; however, given his explosive manner of throwing his opponents to the mat, they soon elevated his nickname to "Thunderduck." Not long thereafter, the wrestling team chose "Thunderduck" as its official mascot name. In 1979, when I became RLC's third president, the college adopted "Thunderduck" not only as its mascot for all sports but also for all students and employees.

You talk a lot about Spirit of Place. How do you share what obviously means a great deal to you with others?

We wanted our students, as well as our employees, to understand that Spirit of Place can be found anywhere throughout their lives and that it is altered for better or worse by each person's behavior in that space. It was important to all of us that students know this history and understand their parts in tapping into and contributing to Richland's Spirit of Place. We incorporated that learning into New Student Orientation, helping students' campus experience literally be a laboratory for daily learning in and out of class.

Water is a huge part of the Spirit of Place at Richland. It is both a powerful life source and a natural resource to be honored and cared for, so it is deeply woven into Richland's student and employee life culture and Richland's story. I wrote the words for this plaque which stands at an important historic spot on the campus:

> **We share Richland's Spirit of Place at this serene spot adjacent to historic waters vital to stone age inhabitants, Caddo and Wichita Indians, Spaniards, and members of the 1830s Peters Colony settlement. This pump honors the well-head of the Caleb Jackson family farmstead whose house stood on this very site from the 1850s prior to the Walton and O'Connor families' deed of this land in 1966 to the Dallas County Community College District for its future Richland College campus, which opened in 1972. As stewards of this land and this legacy, we welcome you to share in the serenity of this site and all that its history holds, as your presence here continues to contribute to its Spirit of Place.**

Water is not only a part of our history; it flows through the heart of the campus. Historic McKamy Springs, a few miles north of Richland's campus became Ferris Creek, which now runs beneath the City of Richardson and emerges as Upper Lake Thunderduck. The water then drips or cascades over a dam adjacent to an outdoor patio and beneath a Student Life atrium building, re-emerging on the other side as a spacious landing with steps that lead gently to Lower Lake Thunderduck, and from there, over another dam at the far edge of the nearly

300-acre campus. Ferris Creek again disappears underground all the way to White Rock Lake—the largest inner-city lake in the USA—and its comingling water eventually passes under the City of Dallas into the Trinity River, the watershed from which water meanders all the way to the Rio Grande, the Gulf of Mexico, and into the oceans of the Earth.

I love that there is both an Upper an Lower Lake Thunderduck. Where else have your used Moby Duck's name on campus?

We built **THUNDERDUCK HALL** in 2003 for the 30th Anniversary. The plaque on that building tells even more of Moby Duck's story:

> ...Richland's unique Thunderduck culture, emanating from the campus' Native American and agrarian origins, is rooted in the belief that it is the whole person who best learns, teaches, serves, and leads. Consequently, our programs and services nurture the integral nature of mind-spirit-body, valuing both emotional and intellectual intelligence.
>
> The first Thunderduck was spotted alongside what is now known as Lower Lake Thunderduck in 1972, when Richland College enrolled its first students but was not recognized as such until 1974, when the duck's thunder species was first identified.
>
> R. Möbius Thunderduck's middle name derives from the principle of the Möbius strip, named for early 19th-century mathematician August Ferdinand Möbius, who formulated the continuous onesided surface formed by twisting one end of a rectangular strip through 180 degrees and attaching it to the other end. With its inner side indistinguishable from its

outer side in continuous movement, the Möbius strip symbolizes for all Thunderducks the vital connection between their inner lives of mind and spirit and their outer reality lives of service to one another, family, community, and our planet and universe.

Thunderduck Hall serves as Richland's front door to the Thunderduck Experience of teaching, learning, and community building.

On behalf of all Thunderducks, "Welcome to Richland College and our best wishes for your every success as a result of your Thunderduck Experience!'

In Karen Jackson's story about her time on your campus, she speaks of the Thunderwater Organizational Learning Institute. Please tell us about that.

Employees named RLC's pervasive required-elective professional development program "Thunderwater" as a physical description of the roaring sound that cascading rain water makes over the central falls throughout the campus and as a metaphor for the awesome power of water and of well-designed and spirited professional development. The Thunderwater Institute has provided the home for much of our Courage and Renewal work.

I have heard that you have a unique way of naming the buildings on campus. Please tell us that story.

In keeping with the Spirit of Place, each building's name begins with a unique mnemonic letter according to its location on campus or primary function inside the building. Then the name is chosen from one of the Texas bodies of water with a Native American, Spanish, or Anglo moniker (the latter associated with the origin of the Lone Star Republic of Texas). Hence Wichita Hall is the primary "generic" classroom building on the West side of the campus; Lavaca Hall is the Learning Resources/Library building; and Bonham Hall houses the School of Business.

Are there any particular buildings or parts of the campus you want us to know about?

One of the newest buildings is **SABINE HALL**, which was built in 2010, uses this Gandhi quote as its inspiration:

My Life is my message.

That seems fitting as Sabine is the facility that is at the core of our effort to become green (we call that GREEEN, which I'll explain in a moment) and environmentally sustainable. Here are my words on the plaque for that building:

> **Sabine Hall was designed and built so that its life would be its message—a message consistent with the vision of Richland College: To be the best place we can be to learn, teach, and build sustainable local and world community.**
>
> **So that our students, faculty, and staff continue to learn, teach, and grow throughout our lives in building sustainable community, Sabine Hall has, to date, become our most tangible symbolic and physical facility at the core of our physical and metaphorical campus, which is the GREEEN Richland Commons:**
>
> **Greening Richland through the Equity-Economy-Environment Nexus is a daily mnemonic reminder, with the 3 E's, that everything we learn, feel, and do regarding sustainable community must hold in**

common the goal to achieve an essential balance of social Equity and justice, Economic viability, and Environmental vitality. Our core teaching-learning organizational approach to achieving our vision is whole-person development and behavior, undergirded by whole-organization behavior in partnership with other organizations and entities to build whole community in an effort to sustain a whole healthy planet.

To these ends, we designed and built Sabine Hall to U. S. Green Building Council LEED Platinum standards, with Sabine's systems and operations minimizing Richland's carbon footprint and its negative impact on the environment, as displayed on monitors that provide daily lessons for our students, faculty, and community stakeholders about the benefits of environmentally healthy facilities that provide cost savings for reinvestment in student instructional programs and services.

Internationally renowned science artist Larry Kirkland's beautiful granite atrium science learning art wall and his granite chiral molecular sculptures flanking Sabine's entrance— designed in consultation with Richland science and art faculty and students— inspire passion about science and sustainable community building, reminding us of the integrated role art and science play in being human, for it is the whole person who best learns, teaches, serves, leads, and lives in sustainable community.

Tell us, please, about the Peace Pole Trail.

Upper and Lower Lake Thunderduck is flanked on the East and West by Richland's buildings and lakeside gardens, outdoor classrooms, and spaces for whole-person meditation. The Peace Pole Trail, which began near the beginning of the 21st century, follows both banks of the lakes, with the 27 poles having been planted on RLC's annual International Student Day, adding a new pole each spring. Each pole is inscribed with the words "May Peace Prevail on Earth" in English and in three of the other languages and dialects spoken by Richland's students from 130 countries, a program now sponsored by Richland's Institute for Peace and Peace Studies Curriculum.

Student stories accompanying the three native languages tell of their experiences from their home country that connect with Richland's sustainable community-building vision during the pole-planting ceremony. Students and employees from across campus and community members participate in each ceremony, frequently accompanied by a parade in and out the entire Trail (Möbius strip-like) from the newest pole past the first pole by the TLC (Teaching-Learning-Community Building) Labyrinth and back, with many of the poles stationed with three representative students in native dress.

The origin of the Peace Pole Trail idea began with a faculty-led 25-member winter retreat to the Fetzer Institute in 1999, which I attended during a walkabout break, I discovered my first-ever Peace Pole in the woods near the ice-covered lake. I immediately shared the idea for our own Richland Peace Pole after the break, when others gave me the history of this worldwide phenomenon, begun in 1955 when I was only 12 years old.

A planned by-product of this retreat was the publication of

participant essays in 2000: *To Teach with Soft Eyes: Reflections on a Teacher/Leader Formation Experience.* Sponsored by the League for Innovation in the Community College (LICC) and the Fetzer Institute, our writing coach English Professor Rica Garcia served as our editor, and Parker Palmer's *Courage to Teach* served as our inspiration. That experience eventually led to the CRWHE becoming an integrating component of Richland's Thunderwater Organizational Learning Institute. At the national level the CRWHE (co-sponsored by the DCCCD and the LICC) continues facilitator development at some 50 American colleges and universities.

How did you incorporate the Touchstones and other formation principles into Richland?

For nearly two decades CRWHE Touchstones have been embedded in Richland's 10 organizational behavioral values for employees and students and therefore in student teaching learning and co-curricular programs: *integrity; mutual trust; wholeness; fairness; considerate, meaningful communications; mindfulness; cooperation; diversity; responsible risk-taking; and joy.* And it is **JOY** ("valuing laughter, play, love, kindness, celebration, and joy in our learning and work—taking our important learning and work seriously and ourselves lightly") that ties these 10 values together at Richland College.

We also embraced the formation principles with such leadership behaviors as starting various council meetings in silence to put aside distractions. Often we would begin with brief appreciative-inquiry stories of students and employees to focus ourselves on what is to be celebrated at RLC, prior to plunging into sometimes challenging, controversial, otherwise potentially divisive agenda items. Similarly, some faculty choose to open their classroom sessions in this manner.

The TLC Labyrinth, the Carillon Tower, the Outstanding Employee Parades, the spontaneous campus-wide Laugh Breaks, and so much more in Richland's culture all emanated from ideas and stories of Richland's pervasive leadership among faculty, staff, students, influenced by Richland's organizational values and reinforced by the impact of the CRWHE campuswide professional development. And every day is punctuated by the quarterly-hour peal of the Carillon Tower, a signal to pause mentally to reflect in gratitude for Richland College and our own teaching, learning, community building activities.

Congratulations on the huge honor of being the ONLY community college to ever receive the prestigious Malcolm Baldridge National Quality Award (MBNQA). We understand that after receiving that award from the White House, you often gave national and international talks about how Malcolm Baldridge's Quality met Parker Palmer's Courage in the way you operated on your campus. Please tell us a bit about that.

Yes, I was honored to receive Richland's Steuben Glass Works Crystal MBNQ Award in 2006, still only the third recipient in higher education. What I loved most about that day was when the video presentation on RLC received a resounding and emotional standing ovation in Washington, D.C., and in Richland's Performance Hall, where it was live-streamed, as I accepted the award on behalf of Richland College Thunder-ducks across the globe.

The White House and U.S. Department of Commerce had sent a media team to Richland months before to create that video. The team really latched onto the Richland College Thunder-duck Spirit of Place as the backdrop for Richland's impressive performance excellence. I still get tears as I remember how the video presentation of Richland's feathered and human Thunderducks at work and play ended with swelling music and the voice-over of Richland's Poet Laureate Jerry McElveen's lyrical paean to the Thunderduck Spirit, inspired by Chaucer's "Parlement of Foules."

And the Thunderduck story continues . . .

Stephen K. Mittelstet is president emeritus of Richland College, DCCCD. He played a founding role at Richland in 1972 – where he established its continuing education program and served on its humanities faculty. Mittelstet served for 30 years as the Chief Thunderduck and was recognized by the 79th Texas Legislature for his outstanding service as president of Richland College and for his contributions to the educational vitality of the state of Texas. Richland also received the Governor's Texas Award for Performance Excellence (the first accredited higher education institution recognized with that honor) and was named a Vanguard Learning College by the League for Innovation in the Community College – several highly-respected honors among a long list of awards and accomplishments garnered during Mittelstet's tenure as president. Today, in retirement, Steve continues to connect soul to role in a personal version of Teaching-Learning-Sustainable Local and World Community Building in his life as a private citizen in his local Dallas and rural East Texas communities and internationally as a Trustee of the International Institute for American Universities, with year-round programs in France, Spain, and Morocco. Steve is a beginning student-apprentice weaver of his own artistic designs – and loves spending time as Gramps with his grandchildren.

The Song in My Heart

By Elaine Sullivan

As I read my colleagues' stories, the song in my heart is one of gratitude: gratitude for the authenticity, the openness, the honesty and the vulnerability expressed in each story.

Shared story invites us to open our hearts, the place where the intellect, emotions, spirit and will converge. In sharing stories, as my colleagues have so beautifully done, we learn to hold a safe space, we learn to let go of judgment, let go of fixing, let go of advice giving, and focus on listening with our hearts. Listening closely to these stories, we hear the themes of the great stories and myths: the call, the journey through darkness, the reclaiming of our gifts and the return to our communities.

Our stories are always changing and fluid.

Beneath the story we know consciously is another story that propels our lives. Making the unconscious part of our story more conscious is life work. In these written stories the evidence of that deep inner work is ever present, the work of listening to our own inner teacher, the work of recovering our True Self. Our stories are written in the biology of our bodies and give us clues to our personal conditioning in mind, body and spirit—clues to who I am.

The stories—narratives and poems—gathered in this book are each a work of art, a work that will continue a lifetime. Through these stories we recognize in a deep and heart-filled way that we are all connected. We discover our similarities and our differences, our uniqueness and our shared humanity.

Through the sharing of these stories, through honoring each person's journey, through deep listening and compassion, we have the opportunity to build caring connections that will continue to enhance our work in this world. To the writers who have gifted the community with these stories – and to the readers who soon may be sharing your own stories, I offer in gratitude this poem written by a dear friend of mine, Macrina Wiederkehr:

I am a vessel of abundant life
a vessel of compassionate presence
a vessel of vibrant hope and affirmation.

I am a vessel of creativity
a vessel of poetry and song
a vessel of stories and dreams.

I am a vessel of joy
a vessel of laughter
a vessel of sorrow
and of tears.

I am a vessel of silence
a vessel of quiet
a vessel of solitude
and deep stillness.

I am a vessel of radical awareness.

The song in my heart is indeed one of gratitude.
You are each a vessel of radical amazement.

Elaine Sullivan is a licensed professional counselor and licensed marriage and family therapist. She is a consultant and has been a facilitator of Courage Work for over 20 years. She prepares facilitators for this work through the Center for Renewal and Wholeness in Higher Education. Elaine lives in Dallas, Texas, and can be contacted at elainemsullivan34@gmail.com – and she invites you to visit her website, www.sullivanconsultingandcounseling.com

AFTER THE STORIES

AFTER WORDS OF APPRECIATION

As we come to the end of gathering the stories for this book, we are overflowing with gratitude for the facilitators and friends of the Center for Renewal and Wholeness in Higher Education (CRWHE), for their courage to go public with their own stories of light and shadow, of brokenness and wholeness. We have special thanks for Sue Jones and Elaine Sullivan and Earlene Bond, without whom this book would not have been possible.

We thank Parker Palmer for his vision that is the ground on which we all stand—and for his generosity in allowing us to share his words.

We thank Donna Bearden for her mandalas and her generosity and her creative-artist soul and her loving story.

We thank John Fox for his beautiful story in this book—and his support of the facilitators of this work over many years, helping us to understand the value of the work he calls Poetic Medicine and its intersection with Courage Work.

And we thank Estrus Tucker who gave us his very precious time while serving as the Interim Director of the Center for Courage & Renewal and shared his heart in his story.

We also hold in our hearts with gratitude a few people who have been very important to this work, but whose stories could not be written for this book. For us, this book could not be complete without including the names of Ann Faulkner and Guy Gooding and Bill Tucker and Garth Hill and Bill Wenrich and Pattie Powell. We feel like we should write the name of Ann Faulkner in all caps—ANN FAULKER!—for her major contributions in the founding of the Center, where she served as the co-director from day one. Sue Jones, the other founding co-director, credits Ann with the success of the Center "from its inception in 2001 as CFCC through the move to Richland in 2007 and beyond."

We have deep appreciation for the many poets and authors and seekers we have quoted in our stories and who have enhanced our journey. (We intentionally made the decision to forego footnotes and bibliographies and to gently embed their names and the sources within our stories. Knowing how deformed we have been by academic writing—and realizing that today's technology has changed our understanding of access to information, we debated whether to use APA or MLA style or some other—and decided instead to create our own! Each writer has shared her or his email or website in the hope that you will reach out with any questions or comments.)

Without Karen Harding, Fay Walker, Don Wells, Sister Mary O'Connor, Bennett and Mary Page Sims, and John Fenner, Karen says she could never have made this journey. And Sally says she has to add both her Life Sisters, Susan and Jane, and her Soul Sisters, Sara and Janet and Sandie and Carolyn E. and Carolyn M. and Trisha, without whom she could not stand in the Tragic Gap.

Words feel inadequate to thank Jim (Sally's husband and forever-love) for always being there, for support and encouragement and design skills and honest words and, most of all, for love. And there are no words to thank Kerri and Jonathan (Karen's children) who encouraged her to pursue her heart work, cheered her on with their love and quick wit, and became "my greatest teachers as I endeavored to live divided no more."

And we thank each other... For saying yes... For always trusting that together, we could be more than either of us could be alone.

With love and courage,
Sally and Karen

WORDS MATTER: OUR GLOSSARY

glos·sa·ry: a collection of textual glosses or of specialized terms with their meanings   (**gloss:** a surface luster or brightness: shine)

----Merriam-Webster Dictionary, 2014

Naming things is a political act, an act of power. So we are naming the things that are important to us—and sharing with you, our Reader, what we mean with the words we use. Words matter, and we want to be inclusive in our language.

We refuse to give up words that are important to us because Others demean them or misuse them or label them as jargon. Instead we are claiming them here. As you read the stories in our book, we hope you'll visit this glossary again and again; bathe in our names for things, delighting with us in knowing what we mean, and seeing the gloss of our words, the shine, the luster.

Birthright gifts: We come into this world as unique individuals, each with our own **birthright gifts**. They are hard for us to see, because they have always been there. Often if something comes easily for us, such as the gift to see with an artist's eye or the gift to remember poetry or solve a math problem or carve a beautiful coffee table, we devalue it. **Birthright gifts** are evident from the moment of birth; we only have to pay attention to an infant to understand that. Babies do not show up as raw material to be shaped by their environment and culture; they come fully formed, with the seed of true self. Yes, we are born with identity and integrity, and even as young children, we know what we like and dislike, what we are drawn towards and what we feel resistance to, what makes us feel alive and what drains our energy. But over the next decade or two, as we move through adolescence and schooling, we too often become **deformed**. We spend the first half of our lives abandoning our **birthright gifts**, Parker Palmer writes in *Let Your Life Speak*, or letting others disabuse us of them. The purpose of education, at its best, is to create the space for each of us to recognize and deepen our unique **birthright gifts**, to honor them and learn to use them in fulfilling our life's purpose.

Boundary markers, touchstones: These are the covenants by which members in circles of trust agree to accept shared responsibility for holding safe and trustworthy space. See **Touchstones.**

Circle of Trust®, circle of trust: The **Circle of Trust®** (capital C, capital T) is a registered trademark for the program grounded in Parker Palmer's writing. Renewal circles, facilitated by CRWHE-prepared facilitators, are often called **circles of trust.** Perhaps even more important, a **circle of trust** (lower case c and t) could be two people or 10 or 20, who create a safe space for the soul to show up. Although you will find other meanings for a **circle of trust** if you search the Web, the best place to understand the phrase as we use in this book is in Parker's writing, especially *A Hidden Wholeness.*

Clearness Committees: The **Clearness Committee** has been adapted for circles of trust from the Quaker tradition. It is a focused microcosm of a larger circle of trust, a safe and trustworthy space, where we have an intense experience of gathering in support of someone's inner journey.

Confidentiality, Deep or double confidentiality: Most of us know the concept of confidentiality, of not sharing anything that is said in a particular setting with anyone outside of those present. **Deep or double confidentiality** is used in the context of the Clearness Committee, meaning that committee members will not speak about what was shared (1) with anyone outside the committee; (2) with each other after the Committee ends; (3) with the focus person about the issue unless she or he requests the conversation.

Courage: From the Latin, *cor,* heart. Courage does not mean that we have no fear, but that we don't act out of that fear. See **heart.**

Courage Work, Courage and Renewal, formation, circle of trust, circles, Reflection and Renewal, Role and Renewal Circles: We have many different ways of talking about the various forms of the work, grounded in the writing of Parker J. Palmer, offered by facilitators prepared by the Center for Renewal and Wholeness in Higher Education. See **circle of trust**.

Facilitator preparation, formation training: The formal program of training offered by the Center for Renewal and Wholeness in Higher Education. See CRWHE in this section for more information and contact Dr. Sue Jones, sjones@dcccd.edu

Focus person: The person who wants clearness on an issue and requests a **Clearness Committee.**

Formation: We have many different ways of talking about the various forms of the work, grounded in the writing of Parker J. Palmer, offered by facilitators prepared by the Center for Renewal and Wholeness in Higher Education. See **circle of trust.**

Going Public: The third stage of Parker Palmer's Movement Model. See **Movement Model.**

Heart: The heart is important in our Courage Work, as it is literally where courage begins. The word courage comes from the Latin word for heart, *cor*. So we are reclaiming the word **heart** from its too-often sentimental use in our culture, to "the core of the self," as Parker writes in *Healing the Heart of Democracy*, "that center place where all ways of knowing converge—intellectual, emotional, sensory, intuitive, imaginative, experiential, relational, and bodily, among others. The heart is where we integrate what we know in our minds with what we know in our bones, the place where our knowledge can become more fully human."

Hidden wholeness: *"There is in all things...a hidden wholeness. This mysterious Unity, and Integrity, is Wisdom, the Mother of all,"* writes Thomas Merton in *Hagia Sophia. "This is at once my own being, my own nature, and the Gift of my Creator's Thought and Art within me, speaking as my sister Wisdom. I am awakened at the voice of my Sister."* Courage work invites individuals who want to live an undivided life into a circle of trust, creating a safe space for the soul to show up, to make that hidden wholeness a bit more visible, to awaken to that inner voice.

Identity and integrity: These two words are at the root of Courage Work, as we talk about creating space where participants can name and claim and nurture their identity and integrity. We share here Parker's beautiful explanation in *The Courage to Teach*: " By *identity* I mean an evolving nexus where all the forces that constitute my life converge in the mystery of self: my genetic makeup, the nature of the man and woman who gave me life, the culture in which I was raised, people who have sustained me and people who have done me harm, the good and ill I have done to others, and to myself, the experience of love and suffering—and much, much more. In the midst of that complex field, **identity** is a moving intersection of the inner and outer forces that make me who I am, converging in the irreducible mystery of being human. By *integrity* I mean whatever wholeness I am able to find within that nexus as its vectors form and re-form the pattern of my life. **Integrity** requires that I discern what is integral to my selfhood, what fits and what does not—and that I choose life-giving ways of relating to the forces that converge within me: do I welcome them or fear them, embrace them or reject them, move with them or against them? By choosing **integrity**, I become more whole, but wholeness does not mean perfection. It means becoming more real by acknowledging the whole of who I am."

Inner Teacher, Inner Voice: The voice of the authentic Self in each of us. Thomas Merton calls it Wisdom (see Hidden Wholeness above).

Listening, deep listening, holy listening: The theologian Paul Tillich said the first duty of love is to listen. A kindergartener named Alec carefully explained to me that the words **listen** and **silent** have the same letters – just in a different order – and you can't do one without the other. Both listening and silence are essential elements of wholeness and renewal circles, and that is where deep listening comes in. Deep listening requires the listener to be fully present, with no necessity to respond or to fix. The purpose is to create the space for the speaker to hear his or her own inner truth. Deep listening may include open, honest questions, which are explained below.

Mobius, Mobius strip, Mobius journey: The dictionary tells us that the Mobius strip, named for the German mathematician A. F. Mobius, is a one-sided surface made by joining the ends of a rectangle after twisting one end through 180 degrees. Parker Palmer talks about the stages of growing into who we are, of developing our birthright gifts, as growing towards "life on the Mobius strip," a seamless flow of our inner life and our outer world. We often talk about our journey to the undivided life as a Mobius journey, a kind-of thin place where inner and outer feel seamless.

Movement Model: See Parker Palmer's *The Movement Way* in The Third Mandala of this book.

Paradox; The ability to understand paradox, to hold two seemingly opposite truths, to embrace both/and rather than either/or, is another important element of the journey toward the undivided life. As the scientist Niels Bohr said, "The opposite of a correct statement is a false statement. But the opposite of a profound truth may well be another profound truth."

Questions, open, honest questions: We have found that questions offer us a much more fertile ground for this journey to living undivided than do answers. The words that Rainer Maria Rilke wrote to a young poet in 1903 still serve as important touchstones for us: "...have patience with everything unresolved in your heart and try to love the questions themselves as if they were locked rooms or books written in a very foreign language. Don't search for the answers, which could not be given to you now because you would not be able to live them. And, the point is to live everything. Live the questions now. Perhaps then, someday far in the future, you will gradually, without even noticing it, live your way into the answer." Honest, open questions have become a practice in our Circles of Trust, one that we learned in the Clearness Committee. Parker defines and teaches the asking of honest, open questions in *A Hidden Wholeness.* He writes that an honest question is one to which the asker cannot possibly know the answer. An open question is one that expands rather than restricts your area of exploration, one that does not push or even nudge towards a particular way of seeing or responding.

Reflection and Renewal: We have many different ways of talking about the various forms of the work, grounded in the writing of Parker J. Palmer, offered by facilitators prepared by the Center for Renewal and Wholeness in Higher Education. See **circle of trust**.

Renewal and Wholeness: We have many different ways of talking about the various forms of the work, grounded in the writing of Parker J.

Palmer, offered by facilitators prepared by the Center for Renewal and Wholeness in Higher Education. See **circle of trust**.

Role and Renewal Circles: We have many different ways of talking about the various forms of the work, grounded in the writing of Parker J. Palmer, offered by facilitators prepared by the Center for Renewal and Wholeness in Higher Education. See **circle of trust**.

Soul: "Nobody knows what the soul is," says poet Mary Oliver in her poem *Maybe*: "it comes and goes/ like the wind over the water." The soul has many names (Thomas Merton calls it true self; the Buddhists, original nature; Quakers, the inner light; Hasidic Jews, the spark of the divine; humanist, identity and integrity)—and Parker writes in *A Hidden Wholeness* that it doesn't matter *what* we name it, but *that* we name it matters a great deal. We have come to know in our renewal and wholeness circles that the soul is shy, making the creation of safe space very important if we are going to have a chance to hear that inner voice.

Third things: Another important practice in our circles is the use of third things so that we don't scare that shy soul away by approaching it too directly. To achieve that indirectionality to help us explore the intersection of our inner and outer lives, we approach topics metaphorically, by using a poem or music or art or quote or object that embodies the themes. Parker names these embodiments as third things—and again, we send you to *A Hidden Wholeness*, if you want more details!

Touchstones: These are the covenants by which members in circles of trust agree to accept shared responsibility for holding safe and trustworthy space. See **The Touchstones** in the first section, *Before the Stories*.

Tragic gap: Parker writes in *A Hidden Wholeness* that "violence of every shape and form has its roots in the divided life." He offers the insight that the heart of nonviolence requires that we acknowledge that we live in a tragic gap—a gap between the way things are and the way we know they might be. In our circles of trust, as we learn to embrace paradox, we also learn the practices that allow us to stand faithfully in that tragic gap, holding the tension between reality and possibility.

The Center for Renewal and Wholeness in Higher Education

The Chambered Nautilus is the emblem for the CRWHE. The chambered nautilus forms its shell and moves into progressively larger compartments as it grows. As each chamber is outgrown, the nautilus walls off its last chamber and lives in the latest and largest one. And yet it remains connected to the earlier chambers by a tube which pierces the walls.

The nautilus navigates by exchanging gas and liquid through the tube. Like the nautilus, a person or [organization] ... is constantly growing, moving into new chambers, closing the door on the past. And yet not utterly. There is always a necessary connection to what we have been, an exchange with the past we use to steer our course ...

[Renewal and wholeness help] us to build more stately mansions to live in, both as individuals and as institutions. The beautiful chambered nautilus is a fitting symbol of continuous growth, of a future that acknowledges and builds upon the past, of the outward manifestation of inner work.

History and Herstory
Gathered by Earlene Bond

In January of 2000, a group of individuals met at the Dallas County Community College District (DCCCD) to explore the seeding, in community colleges across the country, of teacher formation grounded in Parker J. Palmer's Courage to Teach. Included were Mickey Olivanti and Dave Sluyter from the Fetzer Institute; Mark Milliron, CEO of the League for Innovation in the Community College; consultant Monica Manning with Nova Learning; and several individuals from the DCCCD.

The original two-year Courage to Teach seasonal retreat series was created by Palmer at the Fetzer Institute for K-12 teachers in Kalamazoo; four additional pilots had been funded by Fetzer in Seattle, Washington/Baltimore, Kalamazoo, and Coastal South Carolina 1996-1998. The book *The Courage to Teach* was published in 1998.

Fetzer funded the Center for Teacher Formation to offer formation work for K-12 teachers. Now Fetzer was interested in growing the work of formation, and The League for Innovation was attracted to formation as a complement to their other projects, which were mostly technology-oriented. For the DCCCD, this seemed like a next step in their work with formation which included:

-   A six-year relationship with Parker Palmer, extending from 1997 through 2003;

-   Upcoming conclusion of the first two-year Courage to Teach group that included 11 community college faculty and three public school faculty and had been facilitated by Janis Claflin;

- The preparation of six local facilitators, including a former DCCCD chancellor and a community member; and,

- The offering of several introductory sampler retreats, attended by community college and public school personnel.

A luncheon meeting followed in March at the *Innovations 2000* conference of the League for Innovation. Present were Mickey Olivanti of the Fetzer Institute, Mark Milliron and Cindy Miles, VP and COO of the League, and several representatives from the DCCCD. It was decided that a formation retreat for the League representatives of the 20 Board colleges would be the next step to determine interest on the part of these top-tier institutions from across the country.

In July of 2000, that formation retreat was held at the Fetzer Institute's *Seasons*, attended by most of the League representatives, or their designees. Cindy Miles and Cynthia Wilson of the League and Monica Manning also participated. Ann Faulkner and Sue Jones of the DCCCD served as facilitators. Following this retreat, the League and Fetzer decided to partner in this project, and the League asked the DCCCD to be the lead college.

Work began in earnest in late August, and Docket #1856 was approved by the Fetzer Board in December of 2000. Ann Faulkner and Sue Jones were invited to be co-directors of the Center for Formation in the Community College, and Earlene Bond was hired to be the Senior Executive Assistant. The office was located at the DCCCD District Office in downtown Dallas, furnished and equipped by DCCCD. The Center opened on March 5, 2001. Elaine Sullivan joined the Center staff in 2002.

In August 2008 the Center moved to its current location

at Richland College. As CFCC expanded their work from community college teachers to a cross-professional population, they broadened their language from formation to circles of trust and courage and renewal work. CFCC was re-named the Center for Renewal and Wholeness in Higher Education to reflect this broader mission, accepting not only community college faculty, but including higher education faculty as well as others who influenced student learning—librarians, tutors, student services personnel, and many others. Today CRWHE has expanded facilitator preparation to include individuals from many other professions, such as spiritual direction, hospital chaplaincies, and business and industry.

Facilitator Preparation and Other Courage Work: CRWHE Now

Shared by Sue Jones

Since its inception in 2001, CRWHE has prepared aout 200 facilitators. Many of those have come from 45 institutions of higher learning where they help to shape the whole-person/ whole-organization cultures on their campuses. We are currently a small organization that continues to bring the work of renewal and wholeness to the country. We work with wonderful facilitators and facilitators-in-preparation who take the work to their campuses and organizations, and communitites. The numbers of people who they touch are remarkable.

Currently we have a core of three people working within CRWHE:

- **Sue Jones, Director**: Sue may be reached by cell phone almost every day between 10 am and 7 pm Central Time, 940-367-4866 and at sue.jones.klundt@aol.com

- **Earlene Bond, Administrative Assistant:** Earlene works part-time. She is usually in the office on Mondays and Wednesdays, 8 am - 4 pm Central Time. You may reach her at 972-238-6242 or on email, ebond@dcccd.edu

- **Elaine Sullivan, Leading Consultant:** You may reach Elaine at 214-708-3451 between 9 am and 9 pm Central Time. Her email address is elainemsullivan34@gmail.com

Currently we have two events each year:

- We hold a **facilitator preparation retreat** each June in a retreat and b&b facility in the Hill Country of Central Texas.

- We also have a **Gathering** each year in October for facilitators and facilitators-in-preparation. That is a time for all of us who facilitate retreats throughout the year to deepen our understanding of the work of renewal and wholeness. The Gathering is held at one of three community colleges in Texas: North Harris County College in the Houston area; Northwest Vista College in the San Antonio area; and Richland College in Dallas.

- We are available also to facilitate events at your campus or organization. If Sue or Elaine is not available on your dates, we have many experienced facilitators who can step forward.

- We have held a number of pre-conference retreats with great success! If you are a conference planner or know those who are, please recommend us for a pre-conference retreat. Two-and-one-half or three days work best, we are then able to offer Clearness Committees.

We would love to hear from you!

Our Vision: We cultivate communities that serve, where the balance of being and doing is honored and the essence of healthy relationships to self, others, and the earth is sustained.

Our Mission: Our mission is the renewal of whole people who form the heart of whole organizations that are vital to sustaining whole communities.

Our Values: We believe that renewal is an organic, ongoing process that enhances whole people, whole organizations, and whole communities. Our values sustain us and give life to our work.

- Authenticity - We recognize that each person has an inner source of truth—an inner wisdom—that is the basis for the authentic self.

- Wholeness - We honor the unique journey of each individual, one that engages the whole person— mind, body, and spirit—in exploring the inner life.

- Relationships - We value relationships to self and others, acknowledging that inner work is enhanced by being in community, and that self-knowledge enriches our work in the world and our service to others.

- Hospitality - We create a hospitable space, inviting—never expecting or demanding— participation. In this space, participants can speak their truth without fear of judgment or "fixing" from others.

- Mindfulness - We pay attention wholeheartedly to ourselves and others—invoking silence, solitude, and deep listening.

- Trust - We affirm that relational trust is at the heart of our work. We hold each other in trust, neither invading nor evading one another.

- Confidentiality - We maintain a deep confidentiality that honors and affirms the integrity of each person and of the work we do.

- Inclusion - We welcome all to this work. We are enriched by hearing voices of diverse backgrounds and differing perspectives.

ABOUT DONNA BEARDEN:
An Introduction to
CRWHE Friend and Photo-Mandala Artist

Inspired by psychology and spirituality, I became a photo-mandala artist about 10 years ago after careers in public information and educational research.

I have long been drawn to patterns. As a kid, a favorite toy was the Spirograph. The wonder of watching beautiful patterns evolve as I turned a dial was mesmerizing. Kaleidoscopes held a similar fascination. Later I was drawn to geometrical patterns that seemed to get tangled up with art: tessellations, fractals, straight lines that formed curves. In college, photography captured my imagination and I could lose myself for hours in the darkroom, the pull of emerging images holding me in that suspended space of wonder and fascination.

With photo-mandalas, it all came together: photography, mathematical patterns, and my interest in spirituality and psychology. Each mandala is a discovery. Each evokes that childlike wonder that comes from seeing with new eyes. Details hardly noticed in the original photo become magnified and prominent. New images appear as shapes are mirrored and joined. The process of creating photo-mandalas is, for me, a form of meditation.

Almost from the beginning, I paired my mandalas with my writing. What I said with one was magnified or echoed by the other. Mandala Messages became my weekly practice, my thoughts and art going out into the universe. More recently I have begun writing the backstories, sharing the inspiration or experience behind the mandalas.

Please visit my website at www.donnabearden.com to see some of my work and read some of the backstories. If you'd like to receive Mandala Messages once a week, email me at donna.bearden14@gmail.com

THE INSTITUTE FOR

Poetic Medicine

To awaken soulfulness in the human voice

ABOUT JOHN FOX AND POETIC MEDICINE

IPM is a 501(c)3 non-profit dedicated to awakening the healing creative voice inside us. Poetic Medicine encompasses the use of language (spoken and written) as a therapeutic, artistic and transformational medium that connects us more deeply to ourselves, each other, and the universe. Through workshops, training programs, publications, and community building, IPM supports the growing awareness and use of Poetry as a healing tool.

Our Poetry Partner Program provides funding to educators, therapists, community workers, healers, chaplains and poets to provide access to poetic medicine through public projects that reach the marginalized in our culture. Our Poetry Partners serve people in prison along with their families, immigrant and refugee youth, elders in assisted living, persons struggling with addiction, women who have suffered domestic violence and sexual assault, persons living with mental health challenges, college students who seek counseling, people living with traumatic brain injury, and children/teens with physical/developmental challenges.

Our Poetic Medicine Training Program certifies professionals to use poetry and poem-making as a therapeutic and transformational modality.

Over 3 years, this 3-phase low-residency training will give you the direct experience and in-depth training that can make you truly effective in the practice of poetry as healer. To learn more about IPM and our programs, visit our website (poeticmedicine. org) and connect with our community on Facebook

(facebook.com/InstituteForPoeticMedicine/#PoeticMedicine) We offer resources, stories of poetic medicine in action, healing poems, writing prompt suggestions, upcoming events, and news about our poetry partner programs. To be sure you're getting our latest news and hearing about upcoming events in your area, sign-up for our mailing list!

> Poetry is a natural medicine
> that extends solace and relief,
> gives a cathartic voice to suffering,
> reveals insight and shows us what
> it means to be human.
> ~ *John Fox*

Questions? Contact: john@poeticmedicine.org.

YOUR MANDALA:
Offering a few blank pages for your words
and drawings